THOMAS
JEFFERSON

AMERICAN PROFILES

Norman K. Risjord,
Series Editor

American Profiles

THOMAS JEFFERSON

Norman K. Risjord

MADISON HOUSE

Madison 1994

Risjord, Norman K.
Thomas Jefferson

LIBRARY OF CONGRESS CATALOGING-IN-PUBLICATION DATA

Risjord, Norman K.
Thomas Jefferson / Norman K. Risjord. — 1st ed.
p.   cm. — (American profiles)
Includes bibliographical references (p.) and index.
ISBN 0–945612–38–9 (HC : acid-free paper). —
ISBN 0–945612–39–7 (PBK : acid-free paper)
1. Jefferson, Thomas, 1743–1826. 2. Presidents—United States—
Biography. I. Titles. II. Series: American profiles (Madison, Wis.)
E 332.R57   1994
973.4'6'092—dc20
[B]   94–6614
                                                              CIP

Typeset in Fairfield, Berthold Walbaum, and ITC Fenice
Designed by William Kasdorf

Printed in the United States of America
on acid-free paper by Edwards Brothers, Inc.

Published by Madison House Publishers, Inc.
P.O. Box 3100, Madison, Wisconsin, 53704

Contents

Illustrations

Editor's Foreword

THE COMPLAINT OF MANY PEOPLE who dislike history is that it is
full of obscure names, arcane dates, and big words that always
seem to end in "ism." The problem is that history, in some ways,
is like a foreign language. The grammar has to be mastered
before thought, discussion, and interpretation is possible. The
task confronting the teacher of history is how to sugarcoat the
pill.

For some years I have given a talk to educators at meetings
and seminars around the country entitled "Making History Human." It is essentially a pitch for a biographical approach as a
pedagogical device. I am not advocating the reduction of history
to a series of human-interest stories. My thesis, instead, is that
complex and often dry subjects (when presented in general
terms) can be enlivened and given meaning through a focus on
one of the individual stories. For example, P. T. Barnum's impact
on popular amusements can add a new dimension to the concept
of democracy in nineteenth-century America. The story of Jackie
Robinson (or Satchell Paige?) can add poignancy to the often
legalistic (because of its emphasis on statutes and court decisions) story of civil rights in the middle decades of the twentieth
century.

That is the basic purpose of Madison House's *American
Profiles* series—to add a human dimension to the study of history.
American Profiles offers relatively concise and swiftly-paced

sketches that contribute significantly to the discourse on the American past. Each narrative takes advantage of the explosion of recent historiography while the author's interpretive insights serve as a basis for organizing that mass of complex and often disparate information.

What we hope to do with the books in the *American Profiles* series is to tell the American story—to tell the multitude of our national stories. Our goal is to arouse interest and provoke thought. Once that is accomplished, we can truly begin to teach our history.

NORMAN K. RISJORD
Series Editor

Acknowledgments

THIS BOOK WAS CONCEIVED DURING a fishing trip. Greg Britton, director of Madison House, and I were idling away a July morning on a lake in northern Wisconsin when he suggested that I lead off their new American Profiles series with a sketch of Thomas Jefferson. Having been fascinated with Jefferson and the Virginians since my own days at the College of William and Mary, I gladly accepted the challenge. A good historian himself, Greg contributed a number of helpful suggestions that benefited the manuscript.

I am indebted also to the Early American History Study Group at the University of Wisconsin, which did me the honor of devoting one of its sessions to a discussion of the rough draft. I found particularly useful the suggestions of Charles Cohen, John Kaminski, Jean Lee, and Richard Leffler.

Finally, I wish to express my thanks to the anonymous readers whose comments, both prickly and useful, forced me to rethink and recast my interpretation. The book, as a result, is enormously improved. Such people are the unsung heroes of the profession.

N. K. R.
University of Wisconsin–Madison
January, 1994

To my granddaughter, Andrea
whose world, I hope, will be guided
by reason and enlightenment

Introduction

THIS BRIEF SKETCH OF THOMAS JEFFERSON was written simply to acquaint the general reader with the man and his times. It is a digest of existing scholarship, bound together by the theme of Jefferson's evolving philosophy of political economy.

A good deal of ink has been expended in the past on the scholarly debate over the origins of the "Jeffersonian persuasion." Beginning with Bernard Bailyn's *Ideological Origins of the American Revolution* (1967) and culminating with Lance Banning's *The Jeffersonian Persuasion: Evolution of a Party Ideology* (1978), scholars emphasized the influence on Jefferson by English Whig historians, particularly the "Country party" writers of the eighteenth century. These critics, whom Jefferson called "true Whigs," were exercised by the corruption of the age of Walpole, and by "corruption" they meant the management of Parliament through the distribution of offices, titles, and favors. Lance Banning, in particular, argued that Jefferson relied on this Country ideology in building an ideological foundation for the Republican Party in the 1790s.

In the past few years Joyce Appleby and her students have challenged this concept of the "Jeffersonian persuasion." They have argued instead that the form of "republicanism" that Jefferson created in the 1790s represented a complete break with the past—that it was democratic, rather than whiggish, and embraced an economics of free enterprise with equal opportunity for all. Although Jefferson never fully articulated a philosophy of liberal capitalism, he can be seen, in the view of Appleby and her students, as laying the foundation for nineteenth-century capitalist development.

My own feeling is that these two interpretations are not mutually exclusive. Jefferson was not a man of keen introspection; he was fully capable of embracing competing "persuasions" that seem to us today incompatible. His use of Country rhetoric, on the one hand, and the rhetoric of liberal revolution, on the other, was, in my view, a matter of time and circumstance. In his youth he absorbed with zest the writings of the seventeenth-century constitutionalists, Coke and Locke. After he entered politics in 1769, the rhetoric of the "true Whigs" came naturally to him because he saw Virginia society corrupted by British merchants and the web of debt they wove. The Whig historians virtually disappear from his writings after independence, although there are vestiges of Country ideology in the bucolic passages on the virtues of rural life in the *Notes on Virginia*.

Hamiltonian Federalism—with its large national debt, powerful national bank, rampant speculation, and subsidized manufactures—presented an obvious parallel with Walpolean England. That Jefferson and Madison would resort to the idioms of Country party whiggery in building an opposition party was all but inevitable. Nevertheless, as Joyce Appleby has argued, they developed in the course of the 1790s a new vision for American society that involved a complete break with the past because, as Jefferson wrote, the "new principle of representative democracy has rendered useless almost everything written before on the structure of government." His letters of 1800 and the first years of his presidency are full of references to a new age, whether in science, language, or international relations. The staples of Country thought disappear from his writings precisely because that ideology was preoccupied with corruption and government by money. With Republicans in power corruption was no longer a threat.

In the last decade of his life Country party metaphors crept back into Jefferson's correspondence. He was dismayed by the

free-wheeling avarice that characterized the decade after the
War of 1812, and he fretted about the rising political power of
northern businessmen, abetted by the decisions of federal judges
like John Marshall. By the early 1820s Jefferson had come full
circle. He was once more extolling the virtues of the Whig
historians, and he undertook to purge from the University of
Virginia library any writings that he considered "Tory."

In an article in the *William and Mary Quarterly* (October
1993), Peter S. Onuf has suggested that there may be an underly-
ing consensus in the competing interpretations of Jefferson's
ideology. He points out that, although the "liberal" and the
"classical republican" Jeffersons may look in opposite directions,
they shared a sense of the historical significance of the American
Revolution. They also shared a critique of the corruption of the
old regime, whether that be inspired by a liberal vision of the
future or an idealized version of the past. And, finally, both
Jeffersons agreed on the importance of virtue, as well as the
relationship between freedom of enterprise and the public good.
As Isaac Kramnick has pointed out in *Republicanism and Bourgeois Radicalism* (Ithaca, 1990), the middle-class radicals in Britain, with whom Jefferson was intimate both personally and
intellectually, were steeped in the writings of Adam Smith and
the philosophy of laissez faire. Nevertheless, it is my feeling that
any understanding of Jefferson must begin with the realization
that there never was a true "Jeffersonian persuasion," that he
never developed a coherent ideology. He remains an important,
fascinating figure nevertheless. I submit this deliberately brief
sketch of his life in the hope of introducing him to a wide
audience.

THOMAS
JEFFERSON

Thomas Jefferson, portrait in pencil by an unknown artist, formerly thought to have been Benjamin Henry Latrobe. *Courtesy of the Maryland Historical Society, Baltimore.*

Chapter One

───────○───────

Disciple of the Enlightenment

THE PLANTATION HOUSE OF SHADWELL lay nestled in a narrow valley of the Rivanna River, a tributary of the mighty James. It lay in the Virginia Piedmont, within sight of the Blue Ridge, the mountain chain that had intimidated pioneers since their first encounter with it a half century before. It was here, in Shadwell, on April 13, 1743, that Thomas Jefferson was born. His father Peter was already a man of some substance, having served as justice of the peace (a county office with administrative duties that ranged from the care of widows and orphans to road maintenance) and as a member of the colonial assembly. Peter Jefferson had also married well, for Thomas's mother was Jane Randolph, daughter of one of the wealthy planters who had pioneered the migration into the Piedmont a few years before. Thomas Jefferson was born on the American frontier, but the culture that nourished him was centered across the ocean. Absorbing this Anglo-European culture amidst the frontier environment proved to be an intellectual challenge that honed a fine mind into lasting genius.

Virginia had no public schools and few trained teachers. The wealthiest planters sometimes maintained resident tutors, who had been trained in northern colleges or in Britain. Middle-level planters sent their offspring to the local clergyman. Young Thomas had the good fortune to be put in the school of "a correct classical scholar," the Reverend James Maury, an Anglican minis-

3

ter who in 1763 would be the central figure in the "Parson's Cause," a law case that shook the empire and rocketed Patrick Henry to fame. Under Maury's tutelage, Jefferson absorbed Latin and Greek, a bit of literature and mathematics, and, we can be quite sure, heavy doses of the Bible. Despite this childhood exposure, Jefferson was never a deeply religious man. He was a student of the Bible—in later years he had a copy annotated in his own hand—but he treated it as a work of history, rather than the word of God. Jefferson, like his father, would eventually serve on the Reverend Maury's parish vestry, but he never committed himself to the Anglican faith or to any other denomination. He believed in a rational, benevolent God, but he had grave doubts about other aspects of Christian theology. He accepted the teachings of Jesus but rejected much of the writings of the Apostles of the New Testament, as well as the doctrines of the early Christian church. Late in life he would refer to himself as a Unitarian. Maury nonetheless gave his teenage pupil a sound educational foundation. Together with Jefferson's father, the Reverend Maury helped give direction to Jefferson's life, instilling habits of system and industry that would remain with him.

Jefferson was fourteen, and had not yet entered Maury's school, when his father died. His father had been the chief influence on his life to that point, as was customary in the eighteenth century. There was then no concept of childhood as a stage of life. Children were simply miniatures of their parents, to be fashioned into adults by strong discipline. The family arrangement frequently relegated mothers to the role of nurses and housekeepers. Jefferson's mother lived for many years, but by his own reckoning she made no contribution in the shaping of his character or career. Jefferson was fond of the two sisters who were closest to him in age, but he had little in common with three others, who were ten to twelve years younger, or with his brother Randolph, who seems to have been mentally retarded. With the death of his father, Jefferson was effectively alone in the world. It was a measure of his father's training, and the influence of the Reverend Maury, that he continued on the path to fame.

By Virginia custom, and old English law, the lion's share of Peter Jefferson's estate went to his eldest son, Thomas. Peter made provision for his wife and other children, but his will gave Thomas two-thirds of his 7,500 acres, including the land on which Jefferson would later build Monticello. Until Thomas turned twenty-one, executors, designated in his father's will, managed his estate and served as guardians. It was they who, in 1760, granted seventeen-year-old Thomas's request to go to college. There was no discussion as to where he should go. The College of William and Mary, located in the provincial capital of Williamsburg, was the only institution of higher education in the colony, indeed, the only one south of Philadelphia.

Williamsburg was a village of a mere 1,500 people, but it was the first town Jefferson had seen, and the largest one in the colony. Cities, bustling with merchants and artisans, were found in the northern colonies, not in Jefferson's Virginia. Virginia's tobacco planters dealt directly with British merchants or their resident factors. They relied on the mother country for financial services, marketing, and manufactured goods. What they did not import they fabricated themselves on their plantations, using slave artisans. A few villages dotted the map of colonial Virginia, but cities and towns were a thing of the future.

Williamsburg, even so, was a seat of empire, whose authority was little felt in Jefferson's Piedmont, but whose ambitions were nevertheless boundless. Virginia's first charter had given the colony a strip of North America from "sea to sea." On the basis of that, Virginia claimed title to the Ohio River Valley and the Great Lakes. One Virginian even informed an astonished imperial officer that the colony's possessions included "the island of California." The year before Jefferson arrived in Williamsburg, 1759, a consortium of Potomac planters (including George Washington's half-brother) had formed a company to settle a tract of land on the Ohio River.

The College of William and Mary had been founded in part as a training school for clergy of the Church of England, and it was governed by the church when Jefferson arrived in Williamsburg. However, it had never fulfilled its clerical mission because the sons of Virginia planters were more interested in the affairs of this world than in the mysteries of the hereafter. Constantly at war with itself, the College had become little more than an academy serving as a caretaker for the obstreperous youth of the colony. Fortunately for Jefferson, the only member of the faculty who was not a clergyman, Dr. William Small, took a fancy to the gangly youth from Albemarle County. Small had recently arrived from Scotland, a land blooming with the spirit of scientific inquiry of the Enlightenment.

The intellectual climate of the eighteenth century was heavily influenced by the scientific revelations of the preceding age. The discoveries of Copernicus and Galileo concerning the nature of the solar system parted the veil of mystery that had shrouded the mind of the Middle Ages. The notion that there was order in the complex universe, patterns that could be comprehended by ordinary men, marked the transition from the medieval to the modern mind. The English mathematician Sir Isaac Newton completed the transition when he reduced the universe to a uniform system governed by comparatively simple laws of motion. Suddenly the universe was no longer so complex and mysterious, nor subject to unpredictable intervention by the deity; it was consistent, interrelated, rational, and knowable. In the aphorism of one proud English poet: "God said, 'let Newton be,' and there was light." Thus, the leading thinkers of the eighteenth century in Germany, France, and Britain considered themselves "enlightened," no longer bound by the superstitions and habits that had clouded minds and retarded progress. This led to a new spirit of scientific inquiry that ranged from human anatomy to measurement of the size of the solar system. In France "Encyclopedists" sought to catalogue all of human knowledge. In Germany and Britain philosophers attempted to demonstrate the existence of God by rational principles.

Small, who taught mathematics, philosophy, and history, as well as logic, ethics, and rhetoric, imbued Jefferson with this rationalist thought. Small was in fact Jefferson's only regular teacher, and Jefferson continued in his company after he finished college and began the study of law.

Jefferson's decision to enter the law was the result mostly of a lack of any viable alternative. He had no interest in spending his life planting tobacco, and, because of chronically depressed prices, there was little financial reward in farming. He sought a profession that would engage his mind and supplement his income. Entering trade, even if he had possessed a talent for business, was out of the question. Virginia's commerce was managed by British merchants and their resident agents. The ministry was one of the few professions available, but it had little attraction for Jefferson. His interest in religion was academic, not pastoral. Years later he explained to his son-in-law the advantages of the law: "It qualifies a man to be useful to himself, to his neighbors, and to the public. It is the most certain stepping stone to preferment in the political line."

Once again, Jefferson was blessed with an extraordinary teacher. Dr. Small introduced him to George Wythe, a self-educated man who, at the age of thirty-five, was regarded as the most learned attorney in the colony. Wythe was a student of the classics, and in a course of reading that spanned the next three years, Wythe introduced the law to Jefferson as a branch of the history of mankind. Wythe was later a signer of the Declaration of Independence, first professor of law at the College of William and Mary, and an ally of Jefferson's in the reform of Virginia's legal code. They would be life-long friends.

Jefferson's reading in the law helped shape his developing political philosophy. His first brush with history had no doubt come in his father's library where he discovered a copy of Paul Rapin's two-volume *History of England*. Rapin, whose virtues Jefferson extolled to the end of his life, was one of a group of writers that Jefferson called "true Whigs." Rapin found the origins of English liberties in Anglo-Saxon times. The Saxons, an independent, self-reliant and hardy folk shaped by life in the forests of Germany, had brought a system of democratic rule-making to Britain (voting within their clans, for instance, by shaking their spears). Saxon liberties, so Rapin and other Whigs thought, had ended with the Norman conquest of 1066, and the story of English history thereafter was a never-ending struggle between kings who claimed power and people who demanded their rights.

George Wythe reinforced this worldview by introducing Jefferson to the writings of Sir Edward Coke, a seventeenth-century jurist whose *Institutes of the Laws of England* was the fundamental treatise on such vital elements of the law as land tenure. Although a dreary writer, whom Jefferson regarded as "an old dull scoundrel," Coke, as chief justice of the Court of King's Bench, had resisted the theory, borrowed by Britain's Stuart kings from their Continental cousins, that a king ruled by "divine right," that is, the king was the temporal arm of God. Coke dredged up the medieval document known as Magna Carta and made it the cornerstone of English liberties. Contesting the theory of "divine right," Coke advanced the thesis that the powers of the English king were limited, that even the king was subject to the law. Later in the century John Locke and other Whigs would expand Coke's thesis into an English "constitution" that would be a model for American colonists. The notion that the powers of government are limited was central to the American Revolution. In the aftermath of that contest Jefferson attributed many of its ideals to Coke, saying of him, "a sounder Whig never wrote, nor of profounder learning in the orthodox doctrines of the British constitution, or in what were called British liberties."

IN LATE 1765, AT THE AGE OF TWENTY-TWO, Jefferson was admitted to the bar. The process of admission to the legal fraternity in America was more lax than in Britain where the bar (only a "barrister" could appear in court) was as restrictive as a medieval guild. In Virginia each county court was its own bar and imposed its own standards. Patrick Henry, for example, was allowed to practice in the court of Hanover County after only six weeks of desultory reading, although the judge who interviewed him made him promise to read more. It was a measure of Jefferson's intensive preparation, as well as the reputation of his mentor, that he was admitted to the General Court, the highest court in the colony, where the Governor and Council doffed their executive garb and served as judges. Jefferson was no doubt happy to avoid the county courts, where practice involved long hours on horseback riding from one county courthouse to the next.

The General Court met in Williamsburg twice a year, in April and October. Each session lasted for about four weeks. It held a special session in June to deal with contests over land patents. Jefferson always attended this session because petitions involving land patents made up the great bulk of his law practice. Persons could obtain title ("patent") to frontier lands by a grant from the Governor and Council. The only requirement was that the holder "seat and plant" the land within three years and pay an annual quitrent of one shilling per fifty acres. Since much of the land was obtained for speculative purposes, these requirements were often ignored. The only enforcement mechanism was through informers, who could file a caveat ("let him beware") with a court. The first informer to establish that the patent holder was delinquent was entitled to the land. The proceeding was usually adversarial with attorneys representing both sides, and it occupied much of Jefferson's time during his eight years of practice.

Although Jefferson tried his cases in Williamsburg, he was not unfamiliar with the county courts. In 1766 the Governor and Council appointed him one of the judges of the Albemarle County court, a position that he held until 1771. He also frequently attended the court of Augusta County, across the Blue Ridge. The Great Valley west of the Blue Ridge was still in the process of settlement and hence was a fruitful source of land patent litigation. Court day was a social occasion. The whole countryside turned out to collect and pay debts, swap horses and slaves, and look over the wares of itinerant peddlers. Jefferson used the occasion to interview clients and witnesses and search out new business. Blending into the milieu, he gambled occasionally at dice or cards and attended the shows of traveling performers.

Jefferson's account book indicates that he was a busy and reasonably successful advocate. His case load increased steadily until 1773, his last full year of practice, when he handled more than 500 cases. His income, however, was hardly princely. The fee for a common law case before the General Court was limited by law to 50 shillings. Fees in land caveat cases were not regulated, but 50 shillings was Jefferson's usual charge. Collecting the fees was another matter, as a large number of Jefferson's clients failed to pay him. A modern student of Jefferson's account book estimates that his net receipts averaged about £200 a year (about $15,000 in today's dollars). The meager financial returns may explain his gradual loss of interest in the law. He did not even compute the profits from his practice after 1772, and the entries in his case book became shorter and shorter. In May 1773 he joined other lawyers in publishing a complaint in the *Virginia Gazette* about "the unworthy part" of their clients who failed to pay their bills. A few days later his father-in-law died leaving him a fortune (so Jefferson thought) in land and slaves. A little over a year later he turned over 253 unfinished cases to twenty-one-year-old Edmund Randolph, a distant relative and a young man of promise (in 1787 he was elected governor). To the end of his life he was critical of the legal profession, though he continued to value the study of law, as the curriculum and library at the University of Virginia would later attest.

Even at the height of his law practice Jefferson took seriously his obligations as a landowner. Tobacco nurture and slave management were crucial to success as a Virginia planter. Jefferson did that and more; he revolutionized his county's marketing system. Nearly all of Virginia's tobacco was sent to Britain, packed tightly in large wooden barrels called hogsheads. So tightly was it packed that a "middling sort" of planter might see his entire crop jammed into a single cask. Hogsheads, as a result, were very heavy and could be transported feasibly only by water. The most prosperous plantations in Virginia's Tidewater region were located on navigable rivers, where a planter could load his produce on a transatlantic freight vessel. Inland farmers drove an axle through their hogsheads and had a horse drag them to the nearest river landing. Because the Rivanna, which drained much of Albemarle County, was unnavigable when Jefferson came into his inheritance, Albemarle planters rolled their tobacco hogsheads to the point where the river joined the James. Jefferson, with businesslike instinct, saw the drawback in this cumbersome method and traversed the Rivanna in a canoe to identify the obstacles to shipping. He then started a subscription among his neighbors and, with approval of the assembly, got the river cleared. Thereafter, even the planters of Virginia's remote interior had access to the ocean-going ships that docked below the falls of the James at Richmond.

Shortly after beginning his law practice Jefferson felt secure enough to begin construction of Monticello. The land for his "little mountain," to which he gave the Italian name, was part of his father's estate. He planted fruit trees there and began sawing lumber in 1767; the following year he contracted for the leveling of the summit. The architectural concept he obtained from a British architectural manual, which, in turn, was heavily influenced by the work of the sixteenth-century Italian genius Andrea Palladio. Jefferson modified these designs in significant ways. He placed the first floor, which contained the kitchen and wine cellar, underground. Outbuildings, such as stables, storerooms, and slaves' quarters, were likewise placed below the plane of the house, so as not to detract from the visual impact of the main structure. Jefferson adapted the grandiose plans of the European designers to the American environment, and he achieved a structure suitable to a Virginia squire who was soon to reject the pomp of monarchy and aristocracy and embrace instead a simpler, republican society and government. Monticello was a lifelong project, and its changing form reflected the advance of his thought. He remodeled the structure completely in the 1790s, giving it its present appearance, and he was still putting on finishing touches when he was president.

A devastating fire at Shadwell caused him to take up residence at Monticello in November 1770, when only one pavilion of the south wing had been completed. He had but one room, which served as parlor, study, kitchen, and bedroom. About that same time he commenced a courtship which, like the building of Monticello, reflected the surefooted direction he had given his life. The young woman was Martha Wayles Skelton, a twenty-three-year-old widow, who resided with her father near

Williamsburg. Her father, John Wayles, was a lawyer-planter who had amassed a fortune in land and slaves. Martha, his eldest daughter, was the principal heir. She was, of course, a matrimonial prize, and Jefferson had substantial competition for her hand. He won out, it was said, because he shared her love for music. They were married on New Year's Day, 1772, and after the usual festivities Jefferson took her to his cramped quarters at Monticello. The pavilion was known ever after as "Honeymoon Lodge." Their first child, Martha, was born the following September. Over the next ten years the Jeffersons had six children, only two of whom, Martha (Patsy) and another daughter, Mary (Polly), survived infancy. Martha Jefferson herself ultimately died in childbirth in 1782. Jefferson never spoke or wrote of his marriage, and he buried within himself his grief at her death. Yet the marriage was clearly a happy one; domestic peace was ever after at the head of his list of blessings. And he paid close attention to the upbringing and education of his daughters, each of whom married a prominent member of the Virginia establishment. Martha wedded a future governor, Thomas Mann Randolph, Jr., and Mary married a future congressman, John Wayles Eppes.

When Martha's father, John Wayles, died in 1773, she came into possession of the estate, and her husband, by law, had the management of it. It consisted of some 11,000 acres of land and 135 slaves, which doubled Jefferson's wealth. He had two estates in Albemarle County, of which Monticello was the largest. Each was divided into several farms (isolated tracts of land without a residence and usually managed by an overseer). Seventy-five miles to the southwest were several other farms, on one of which he eventually built an estate house, which he called Poplar Forest. On his Albemarle farms Jefferson was already switching from tobacco culture to wheat and other grains, but he continued to grow tobacco on the more newly opened lands in the southwest until late in his life. Less than half of his land was under cultivation. Although Jefferson felt that tobacco was more ruinous to soil than wheat, the fact was that both crops exhausted a piece of land within a few years. Fertilization was a known but expensive practice. It was more economical to let an exhausted tract lie fallow for a few years, while cattle, hogs, and wildlife, which fed on the weeds and brush, restored its fertility. Much of the land was too steep to cultivate at all. As late as 1815 a traveler estimated that half of Monticello's thousand acres was "covered with a noble force of oaks in all stages of growth and decay . . . abandoned to nature." That form of land use was also vitally important to Jefferson.

Along with Wayles's extensive landholdings, Jefferson inherited his sizable debts to British merchants. While Jefferson sold half of Wayles's lands in an effort to pay off these debts, the series of transactions broke down during the Revolution. The purchasers paid him in Revolutionary paper money, which was almost worthless in Virginia and utterly unacceptable to British merchants. Jefferson ultimately paid Wayles's debts twice and did not profit much from the inheritance.

IN THE MEANTIME, JEFFERSON HAD BEGUN THE SHIFT from law to politics. It did not necessarily involve an abandonment of the law; he would instead devote his legal skills to the building of a nation. The path to power in colonial Virginia was a ladder of preferment. The first rungs were local offices, the church vestry, the county court. After proving himself at that level the political aspirant would be elected to the House of Burgesses, the lower house of the assembly and the highest elective office in the colony. Success there could lead to election as Speaker of the House or an administrative office, such as treasurer of the colony. With enough wealth, experience, and influence, a Virginian might be named to the governor's council, an office appointed by the king's privy council on the advice of the governor. Jefferson's father had pursued this route as far as the House of Burgesses. Jefferson reversed the process by starting in the Burgesses, winning election to that office in 1769. Four years later he picked up the loose threads by serving as vestryman and justice of the county court.

The House of Burgesses was, as one historian has said, "a tobacco planters' club." The qualifications for admission were family status, wealth, and genteel manners. The most powerful members, with surnames like Byrd, Carter, and Randolph, could trace their lineage to seventeenth-century ship captains and merchants. The unspoken rule was that it took more than one generation to make a gentleman. The House was also a cousinship, for the members were nearly all related to one another through family alliances sealed by marriage. Jefferson, however much he differed from his fellow delegates in mind and temperament, was a member of the club. When he entered the House he could count a half dozen blood relatives. The delegates were also in common agreement about the relationship between Virginia and the mother country. As early as 1759 one observer wrote of the Virginia gentry: "They are haughty and jealous of their liberties, impatient of restraints, and can scarcely bear the thought of being controlled by any superior power. Many of them consider the colonies as independent states, unconnected with Great Britain otherwise than by having the same common king." Ever since Bacon's Rebellion nearly a century before, Virginians had seized upon English Whig theory that the powers of the king were limited, and they had given it an American spin. They contended that the power of both king and Parliament, as well as their agents in America, the royal governors, was limited by historical precedent and natural law.

Despite the chummy atmosphere, the House of Burgesses was a troubled body in the late 1760s. Its distress reflected a larger malaise among the planter gentry it represented. The pattern of Virginia's tobacco culture had been changing since the 1730s, to the disadvantage of the planters. Since the late seventeenth century large planters with access to the sea had dominated the market, collecting the produce of their inland neighbors and sending the annual crop on consignment to London merchants. About 1730 Glasgow firms began to enter the tobacco trade, operating through agents or "factors" who resided in Virginia. These Scottish factors penetrated into the interior, offering top prices for tobacco and generous lines of credit for the opening of new lands in the Piedmont. The direct export of tobacco to Glasgow, and from thence to the continent of Europe,

"The Forest," home of Jefferson's father-in-law, John Wayles. Most Virginians, even those with extensive holdings in land and slaves, lived in rather modest farmhouses. *Courtesy of the Valentine Museum, Richmond.*

bypassed the seaboard planters and threatened their position in Virginia's economy and society. The "middling" planters of the Piedmont initially benefited from the expansion of credit, but they soon found themselves deeply in debt to British merchants. The result was that the entire colony became caught in a cycle of dependence and debt—dependence on a single-staple economy, on a foreign market, and on British credit. Relatively good prices for tobacco in the 1740s and 1750s obscured the problem, but a severe depression in the mid-1760s brought home to Virginians the fact that they had lost control of their lives and fortunes.

Virginians feared that a seemingly permanent debt destroyed their personal independence and moral fiber, thus threatening the social and political stability of the colony. Although they accused the British merchants of depressing the price of their tobacco and imposing a markup on manufactured goods they purchased, Virginians also blamed themselves for their plight. John Wayles, soon to be Jefferson's father-in-law, complained in 1766 that "Luxury and expensive living have gone hand in hand with the increase of wealth." Added another planter a few years later, the "Root of our misfortunes is our Pride, our Luxury and Idleness." In the midst of the mid-1760s depression a political scandal confirmed the relationship between indebtedness and moral laxity.

For two decades a handful of men with such formidable surnames as Carter, Nicholas, and Randolph, had dominated the assembly and monopolized the executive offices. The most powerful of these was John Robinson, who was both Speaker of the House and treasurer of the colony. When Robinson died in 1766 it was discovered that he had embezzled £100,000 in Virginia currency and distributed it among friends. The scheme reflected an early version of machine politics rather than outright dishonesty. Virginia had financed the French and Indian War by issuing paper money, intending to retire the debt after the war by collecting the paper in taxes and burning it. However, Robinson, as treasurer, did not destroy the money. Instead, he loaned it to friends who had found themselves in financial trouble in the postwar depression. Robinson expected them to repay the loans, and from these proceeds he would reimburse the treasury. Unfortunately, he died before this could be done.

Some 240 planters took advantage of the offer, including Jefferson's father and future father-in-law. With so many beneficiaries the embezzlement could hardly have been a secret. Even so, it might have been kept within the gentlemen's club but for two newcomers, Patrick Henry and Richard Henry Lee. Both were sons of self-made gentlemen, as Jefferson was, and both resented the tightly knit oligarchy that controlled the assembly. Patrick Henry had entered the House of Burgesses in 1765 and leaped to instant fame with his Stamp Acts resolves, which denied that Parliament had any power to tax American colonists. Lee entered the Burgesses a year later and quickly made the

Robinson affair his personal crusade. In Lee's mind the scandal represented the sickness of Virginia society. Virginians, he thought, had succumbed to luxury and indulged themselves in foreign goods far beyond their means to pay.

AS PART OF THE PROTEST AGAINST THE Stamp Act, northern merchants had refused to buy British goods. Led by Henry and Lee, Virginians enthusiastically joined the boycott. They hoped not only to force a repeal of the legislation but to encourage economic diversity that would free the colony of dependence on British merchants. By voluntarily depriving themselves of British goods, Virginians hoped to encourage domestic manufactures. In a letter to his London merchant in September 1765, George Washington predicted that the development of domestic manufactures would lead Virginians to realize "that many of the Luxuries which we have heretofore lavished our Substance to Great Britain for can well be dispensed with whilest the Necessaries of Life are to be procured (for the most part) within ourselves." In the spring of 1766 Parliament yielded to the American protest and repealed the Stamp Act. It sought to establish its constitutional position (as well as save face) by adopting a Declaratory Act, which stated that Parliament had the naked, if at the moment unexercised, power to tax the colonies. Parliament's repeal of the Stamp Act seemed to vindicate Virginia's action. The Burgesses were prepared to resort to economic retaliation again when Parliament challenged it anew—with the Townshend taxes of 1767.

The Townshend taxes originated in a misconception. Stunned by the violence of the American protest against the Stamp Act, Parliament called upon Benjamin Franklin, colonial agent for Pennsylvania, for information. Franklin testified that the objection to the Stamp Act was that it was an excise, a tax on goods and services produced within the colonies. Such taxes had traditionally been the domain of the colonial assemblies. The implication of Franklin's position was that external taxes, duties on items imported into the colonies, would be acceptable. With more than a dose of cynicism, Chancellor of the Exchequer, Charles Townshend, decided to test this thesis. In 1767 he proposed an assortment of duties on goods that the colonies imported, such as glass, paper, and tea. The cynical feature of the act was that the expected revenue was paltry. Thus, the true purpose of the taxes was political—to establish Parliament's right of taxation. As if to taunt the colonists further, Townshend's measure earmarked some of the revenue for the payment of salaries of royal governors, thereby freeing them from their financial dependence on colonial assemblies.

The Townshend taxes drove the colonists another notch toward Revolution. A circular letter, drafted by Samuel Adams and approved by the Massachusetts assembly, denied that Parliament had any authority to tax Americans, internally or externally, because Americans had no voice in Parliament. Nonimportation associations sprang up in northern seaports, binding merchants in a boycott of goods subject to the tax. The royal government's response was to denounce the Massachusetts circular letter and to order governors to dissolve any assembly that approved it.

Such was the imperial crisis when Jefferson made his appearance in the House of Burgesses at the beginning of its May 1769 session. Jefferson had already met Patrick Henry, who was four years older. As a college student Jefferson had stood at the assembly door during the Stamp Act debates and listened to Henry's famous speech. Although Henry probably did not conclude the speech with the oft-quoted exhortation "If this be treason, let us make the most of it," Jefferson recalled later that Henry "appeared to me to speak as Homer wrote." On entering the Burgesses Jefferson immediately allied himself with the Henry–Lee radicals.

At the outset of its session the House unanimously passed resolutions asserting that only the colonial assemblies had the power to tax Americans and affirming the right of the colonies to take united action in securing a redress of their grievances. The governor summoned the House to attend him in the council chamber and dissolved it. Undaunted, the ex-burgesses assembled in the Apollo Room of the Raleigh Tavern, a few blocks up Duke of Gloucester Street from the capitol, and adopted a nonimportation association, the framework of which was drafted by Washington and his Northern Neck neighbor, George Mason. Subscribers to the association agreed not to purchase or consume a wide variety of British goods in addition to those taxed by Parliament. Among the items boycotted were leather goods, including boots and shoes, food products and liquor, and all forms of British finery, including silks, fabrics from India, ribbons, and stockings. The association permitted Virginians to import coarse cottons and woolens, which planters needed to clothe their slaves. The purpose thus was to encourage manufacturing and economic diversity, in addition to putting political pressure on Parliament. Unfortunately the Virginia association was purely voluntary, unlike those in the North which were enforced by the Sons of Liberty and their female counterparts, and it soon collapsed. The Scottish factors refused to cooperate from the outset and in fact used it as an opportunity to expand their business. Virginia imports actually increased in 1769 and 1770, fueled by a dramatic expansion of British credit. Virginians found themselves deeper in debt than ever. The nonimportation agreements nevertheless had the desired effect. In 1770 a new ministry under Frederick Lord North repealed the taxes, with the exception of the duty on tea, which was retained as a symbol of Parliament's right to levy taxes.

When news of the repeal reached Virginia, no one greeted the announcement as an American victory. Although relieved of parliamentary taxation, they were still at the mercy of British merchants, whose actions had helped undermine Virginians' political rights. Concluded one great planter, "We must work our own deliverance which is in our power. I think we must depend merely on our own conduct and Resolution, to import Nothing but what is absolutely necessary." In June, a popular meeting in Williamsburg, including former Associators, members of the House of Burgesses, and a large number of merchants, formed a new Association. This one would be enforced by a committee of five in each county. It greatly expanded the list of prohibited British goods, and it established a price ceiling on tools, implements, and clothing that Virginians needed. Unfortunately, the Scottish factors habitually stocked their stores with the cheaper goods, and the Association had no effect on them. As a result, it soon collapsed. Jefferson was elected to the Albemarle County enforcement committee, but by early 1771 he could foresee the Association's demise. He ordered his London agent to ship some prohibited goods because a dissolution of the Association was likely by the time the ship arrived.

The nonimportation experiment revealed the divisions within Virginia. The great planters, who traded directly with London merchants, supported the Association. Scottish factors and their customers, the "middling" planters, had ruined it, with the help of easy credit in the mother country. The credit boom ended suddenly in 1772, causing a number of British firms to fail and tobacco prices to plummet. In the ensuing depression all segments of Virginia society faced financial ruin. Small tobacco producers at last learned how disastrous was their dependence on Scottish factors. Their interests fused with those of the planter gentry and resident merchants who for years had been trying to establish some degree of economic independence from Great Britain. When the confrontation with Parliament resumed in 1774, Virginians were united as never before. Jefferson drew two lessons from the experiment in commercial retaliation. One was that economic freedom was the basis of political freedom, and political liberty could be sustained only by economic diversity and enterprise. The other was the realization that trade was a potent weapon in international relations. Throughout the rest of his long political life he considered commercial retaliation a sword in the defense of American rights.

The repeal of the Townshend taxes in 1770, together with adroit handling of the Boston Massacre by the governor of Massachusetts, defused the imperial crisis for the moment. Jefferson used the respite to immerse himself further in the political thought of the Enlightenment. The most widely read work of the time was the eleventh book of the *Esprit des Lois* by Baron de Montesquieu. An admirer of the British constitution and limited monarchy, Montesquieu portrayed it as the modern model of "balanced government." The theory of balanced government originated with Aristotle, who thought that government should represent the three orders of society—royalty, nobility, and populace. Left to itself, each element led to ruin: despotism, oligarchy, or mob rule. But in tandem they balanced one another, providing stability with benefit to all. Applying this classical theory to the contemporary British government, Montesquieu contended that the British government was the most stable, and the freest, in the world because of the balance of power among king, lords, and commons. Jefferson read the *Esprit des Lois* in 1770, and it earned twenty-seven entries in his legal commonplace book, more notes than he made on any other book or author. After the Revolution, when he realized that "balanced government" meant the preservation of a social and political elite, he would reject Montesquieu, but in the early 1770s the French philosopher's thesis was grist for his mill. Jefferson embraced Montesquieu's ideas because they blended with his earlier reading of John Locke. Writing in the late seventeenth century, Locke had been the principal critic of the theory of "divine right," and he had posited Parliament as the principal watchdog for the rights of citizens.

Reinforcing the theories of Locke and Montesquieu were the political disquisitions of English Country writers, "true Whigs" Jefferson called them, whose works he began to collect while in college. The problem, as perceived by these writers, was that Parliament had ceased to be the guardian of liberty and had succumbed to corruption. Under the control of Whigs, following the Hanoverian succession to the throne in 1715, Parliament became the locus of political power. The Whig prime minister, Sir Robert Walpole (1721–1742) allied himself with the money and banking interests of London and controlled Parliament through a judicious distribution of favors, titles, and offices. Rural gentry resented this corrupt union of political and financial power, and their spokesmen (ranging from the Tory Viscount Bolingbroke to the "true Whig" Catherine Macauley) amended the old Saxon theory of English history. Although the struggle against the Stuarts culminating in the Glorious Revolution of 1688 had ended any danger of arbitrary rule by the Crown,

Parliament, they argued, posed a new problem. Parliament was no longer the watchdog of liberty because Parliament itself could be manipulated and governed. The danger was more subtle, but it was no less frightening because corruption had spread outside the government and permeated the whole society.

The alarm of the Country writers, and that of Americans like Jefferson who read them, increased with the accession of King George III in 1760. Determined to resurrect the influence of the Crown, George III had rid himself of the Whig grandees and adopted as his own their style of governing. By distributing offices and royal favors, the king had created his own "party" in the House of Commons, known as the "king's friends," and he had rendered the old party labels, Whigs and Tories, obsolete. Having wrecked the British model that Montesquieu so much admired, George III was extending his tentacles over America. Or so Jefferson believed. The solution was to reject the authority of Parliament and to reform the king. A new British provocation, popularly known as the "tea act," presented Jefferson with an opportunity to expound his emerging philosophy.

The tax on tea, the lone survivor among the Townshend taxes, was widely evaded, not only in America, but in Britain itself. Because of the high duty on tea imported by the British East India Company, tea brought from Asia by the Dutch was smuggled into both mother country and the colonies. The British East India Company suffered from the loss of business, and by the end of 1772 it was on the verge of bankruptcy, unable to sell the huge surplus of tea in its warehouses. In May 1773 Parliament came to the company's rescue with an act permitting it to dispose of its tea in America through its own agents. By eliminating mercantile middlemen, the British tea could compete with Dutch tea, and the East India Company could recoup its fortunes. Although tea was still subject to a special tax in America, Parliament did not anticipate any trouble from Americans.

The colonists, however, instantly viewed the measure as a plot to induce Americans to purchase dutied tea and thereby admit the right of Parliament to tax. Benjamin Franklin, coming to the close of his career as a colonial agent in London, labeled

Lord North's policy as an effort to "overcome all the patriotism of an American" by offering him cheap tea. The reaction was most violent in Samuel Adams's Boston where the arrival of an East India Company tea ship precipitated a "Tea Party" at which the tea was dumped into Boston harbor in December 1773.

During the annual meeting of the Virginia assembly in the spring of 1773, Jefferson, Patrick Henry, the Lee brothers, and other "hot heads" met privately and agreed to a series of resolutions calling for the creation of committees of correspondence to facilitate communication among the radical elements in each colony. Committees of correspondence were already functioning in Massachusetts, but Jefferson thought that the resolutions drafted by his group and passed by the House of Burgesses were the first that looked to an intercolonial network. The governor terminated the assembly when he learned of the resolutions, but the committees were soon in place.

Through the committees of correspondence, supplemented by a private exchange of letters between Samuel Adams and Richard Henry Lee, the Virginians were kept abreast of the resistance movement in Massachusetts. By the time the Virginia assembly reconvened in May 1774, Parliament had retaliated against Massachusetts for the Tea Party by suspending its charter, placing it under military rule, and closing the port of Boston. Virginians and other colonists perceived these "intolerable acts" as a renewed threat to their own self-government. When the House of Burgesses met in May 1774, the radical cadre "cooked up a resolution," as Jefferson phrased it, appointing the first day of June, the day the port of Boston was to be closed, as "a day of fasting, humiliation, and prayer" that would "turn the hearts of the king and Parliament to moderation and justice." When the House unanimously passed the resolution, the governor, by knee-jerk reflex, dissolved the assembly. The burgesses reconvened at the Raleigh Tavern and proposed a continental congress to meet in Philadelphia on the first of September. They also recommended that the counties elect delegates to a convention to meet in Williamsburg in August for the purpose of adopting a new trade embargo on British goods.

Although the Association adopted at Williamsburg did not meet the desire of some for a complete economic break with Britain, it was the most elaborate response of any colony to Boston's call for a boycott of trade. It also served as a blueprint for the Continental Association approved by the Continental Congress in Philadelphia that autumn. The Williamsburg convention concluded its work by electing delegates to the Continental Congress. Jefferson might have been included in this delegation, but he had fallen ill on the road to Williamsburg and failed to take his seat in the convention. Nevertheless, from his sick bed, he forwarded to convention chairman Peyton Randolph some instructions to guide the delegates sent to Philadelphia. The convention thought his essay too bold to serve as instructions, but friends published it privately under the title A Summary View of the Rights of British America.

A Summary View began with the proposition, voiced by Colonel Isaac Barry during the debates over the Stamp Act in the House of Commons, that Americans were "sons of liberty," that they had fled England initially in search of freedom and had created a new society in America geared to the general happiness. Jefferson then listed the many encroachments of the Crown and Parliament on American rights. The core of his complaint was that Parliament's regulation (he called it "tyranny") of American commerce was an infringement of the colonists' natural right to free trade with all nations. Since the mid-seventeenth century, Jefferson wrote, Parliament's navigation acts had restricted American trade with the sole object of lining the pockets of British merchants. He recommended that the Continental Congress declare all such acts void. It was the broadest assertion yet heard in Virginia of the rights of American colonists. Although Jefferson's pamphlet is sometimes viewed as a clarion call for the "rights of man," Jefferson did not concern himself, at this point, with the rights of individuals. A Summary View focused instead on the "right" to govern—that is, the unfair distribution of power in the colonial relationship between Britain and America. Jefferson concluded with a vague hint that the solution may be independence for America: "The God who gave us life gave us liberty at the same time; the hand of force may destroy, but cannot disjoin them."

Although it had little impact on the king, *A Summary View* earned Jefferson an intercolonial reputation as a political radical, and one who possessed a facile quill. Nearly two years later, after the Revolution broke out, the Congress would ask him to draft its Declaration of Independence.

Chapter Two

Catalyst for Reform

ROYAL AUTHORITY EVAPORATED in almost every colony after violence erupted at the battles of Lexington and Concord in Massachusetts in April 1775. Virginia's governor, Lord Dunmore, took refuge aboard a British man-o'-war in the York River. From there he issued a proclamation urging slaves to rise up against their masters and join the British cause. A few African Americans did respond to the governor's call in the hope of winning their freedom, but the governor's proclamation effectively ended any influence he had among white Virginians. Committees of safety sprang up in every county, and the House of Burgesses, which had followed a political path similar to Jefferson's in the preceding decade, transformed itself into a revolutionary convention directly representing the people. Jefferson himself marveled at the ease with which Virginia slipped into self-rule. In August 1777 he wrote Benjamin Franklin:

> With respect to the state of Virginia in particular, the people seem to have deposited the monarchical & taken up the republican government with as much ease as would have attended their throwing off an old & putting on a new suit of clothes. Not a single throe has attended this important transformation. A half dozen aristocratical gentlemen agonizing under the loss of preeminence have sometime ventured their sarcasms on our political metamorphosis. They have been thought fitter objects for pity than punishment.

The Second Continental Congress met in Philadelphia on May 10, 1775, and the Virginia convention added Jefferson to its delegation. On June 21, he joined the assemblage that was meeting in the Pennsylvania State House (Independence Hall). Jefferson's reputation preceded him. John Adams noted that Jefferson brought to Congress "a reputation for literature, science, and a happy talent of composition." Jefferson was at once drawn to the crusty New Englander, whose politics were identical to his own. In the First Continental Congress the previous September John and his cousin Samuel Adams had found allies among the Virginia delegation, notably Patrick Henry and Richard Henry Lee. The "Adams–Lee Junta" was at the forefront of the radical element in the Second Congress, and Jefferson was a ready recruit. The talents of Henry and Lee were mainly oratorical, and Jefferson let them handle the speechifying. His mark would be made with his pen. But he was also active behind the scenes. "Though a silent member of Congress," Adams said of him, "he was so prompt, frank, explicit, and decisive upon committees and in conversation, not even Samuel Adams was more so, that he soon seized upon my heart."

Despite the outbreak of fighting, a line of communication with the mother country remained open, and a flurry of petitions, manifestos, and "Olive Branches" crossed the Atlantic during the summer and fall of 1775. Jefferson served on several committees that drafted Congress' response to the royal overtures. By the end of the year, however, it was evident that there could be no reconciliation. In January 1776 the publication of Thomas Paine's pamphlet *Common Sense* focused the growing feeling that the only reasonable outcome of the Revolution was independence.

Jefferson spent the early months of 1776 at Monticello, detained initially by the illness of his wife and then by an "inveterate headache" of his own. (Jefferson would suffer periodic bouts of migraines throughout his life.) By the time he took his seat in Congress on May 14, 1776, a number of steps had been taken toward independence. Congress had established a secret committee to seek foreign aid, authorized privateering, and opened American ports to non-British trade. The day after Jefferson took his seat, Congress approved a motion by John Adams encouraging the colonies to establish their own governments. That same day, May 15, the Virginia convention unanimously instructed its delegates to propose a declaration of independence. Not waiting for Congress, the convention declared Virginia's independence and set about drafting a constitution for the new state.

On June 7, 1776 Richard Henry Lee responded to the convention's instruction by offering a resolution stating that the colonies "are and of right ought to be, free and independent states." The resolution also proposed a continental union and foreign alliances. When Congress took up the resolution on the following day, Jefferson recorded the arguments for and against. As usual, the Massachusetts–Virginia axis favored immediate action, contending that independence was already a fact. Delegates from the middle states and South Carolina urged delay. They argued that their constituents were not quite ready for so radical a move, and their state assemblies had not authorized them to vote for independence. The dispute ended in compromise. Congress delayed a vote on the resolution for three weeks, and in the meantime it named a committee of five to draft a declaration. On the committee were Jefferson, Adams, Benjamin Franklin, Robert R. Livingston of New York, and Roger Sherman of Connecticut.

The committee met, perhaps without Franklin who was suffering from gout, and Jefferson agreed to prepare the draft. Adams later recorded an exchange that began with Jefferson's asking him to write the document, and in which Adams replied:

"Oh! no."

"Why will you not. You ought to do it."

"I will not."

"Why."

"Reasons enough."

"What can be your reasons?"

"Reason first—you are a Virginian, and a Virginian ought to appear at the head of this business. Reason second—I am obnoxious, suspected, and unpopular. You are very much otherwise. Reason third—You can write ten times better than I can."

"Well, if you are decided I will do as well as I can."

Adams's recollection may not have been accurate in every detail, but it is the best explanation we have for how Jefferson came to be the author of the Declaration of Independence. And the tale is a fixture of American lore.

Jefferson drafted the declaration in his quarters on the second floor of a brick house at Second and Market streets. His primary purpose, as expressed in the opening paragraph, was to explain to the world the reasons for the colonies' separation from Great Britain. But he used the occasion to advance a rational, enlightened foundation for the government of the new nation. The second paragraph, the most celebrated feature of the Declaration, is a syllogistic argument beginning with the "self-evident truth" that all men are created equal. They are equal because each possessed certain "unalienable rights," rights endowed by their "Creator," not wrung from some grudging monarch. Then the trenchant conclusion: "to preserve these rights governments are instituted among men." Government, then, existed not for the glory of the king or the pomp of empire; its primary purpose was the preservation of human rights. To insure that it adhered to this purpose, it derived its authority from the "consent of the governed." In this single paragraph Jefferson wove together the elements of modern government—the Enlightenment principle that governmental legitimacy could be founded on reason and did not depend on history; the republican principle that people could select their rulers and not be dependent on the accidents of royal birth; and the democratic principle that political authority derived from the consent of the governed.

Jefferson then launched into a lawyer's brief on the misdeeds of the king. He directed his attention at George III, rather than Parliament, because Congress had already denied the authority of Parliament over America; allegiance to the king was the last thread holding the empire together. He had rehearsed the list of accusations in his *Summary View*. The list of eighteen complaints was designed as *prima facie* evidence that the king had destroyed the rights of the colonists, and, pursuant to Lockean theory, Americans had a right to "institute new government." With a superb rhetorical flourish, Jefferson ended the declaration with a pledge that its signers would sacrifice, if necessary, "our lives, our fortunes, and our sacred honor."

The committee made only a few modest editorial changes and sent the document to the floor of Congress. Congress heard it read on June 28 but tabled it pending the disposition of Richard Henry Lee's resolution on independence. By the end of June radicals in Pennsylvania, having seized control, authorized independence, and South Carolina's wealthy planters had yielded to the political tide. Lee's resolution was approved on July 2 with only New York, whose delegates pled lack of instructions, in opposition. Congress then took up the declaration, debating it line by line for two and one-half days. Unaccustomed to editorial scrutiny, Jefferson squirmed in his seat. Nevertheless, it must be said that Congress strengthened the document. It tempered some of Jefferson's more extreme denunciations of the king, and it corrected some of Jefferson's history. It eliminated altogether, for instance, Jefferson's denunciation of the king's "cruel war against human nature itself" by the traffic in slaves. Clearly, Congress recognized that Americans were as guilty as the British in the crime against Africa. New Englanders were much involved in the slave trade, and southerners had eagerly purchased the human chattel.

Even so, Congress missed the point that Jefferson was trying to make, understandably enough because Jefferson's argument was uniquely Virginian. Virginia Patriots who wanted to sever the imperial tentacle that kept them in perpetual debt recognized that slavery was at the root of their tobacco culture. The heavy investment in their labor force effectively prevented them from diversifying their economy beyond agriculture. Moreover, the easy credit of the late 1760s had allowed Piedmont planters to expand their slave labor force, thus extending the area of tobacco culture and the commercial bondage of white Virginia. The Nonimportation Association of 1770 included an article forbidding the further import of slaves. Like the other features of that Association, the ban was not enforced, but the House of Burgesses maintained an opposition to the slave trade even in the

In this rough draft written in June, 1776, Jefferson worked out the wording of the Declaration of Independence. He later chafed at Congress's editorial intervention. *Courtesy of the Library of Congress.*

boom years of 1770–1772. Because the British government would not countenance an abolition of the slave trade, the assembly tried several times to double the tax on imported slaves. Its efforts were thwarted by the Board of Trade, which instructed Virginia's governors to reject any such move. This was the burden of Jefferson's complaint in the Declaration of Independence. He was, to be sure, sickened by the inhumanity of the slave trade. But in ascribing reasons why the peoples of Britain and America should sever their relationship, he could not refrain from raising once again the issue of America's commercial freedom.

Adopted on the evening of July 4, 1776, the Declaration was read to an assemblage of Philadelphians in the State House yard two days later. Before the signing was complete—the New York delegation was still awaiting instructions—General George Washington was having it read to the soldiers of the Continental army. The Declaration gave new force to the Revolution, and it opened a new era for mankind.

It was some years before Jefferson's authorship was widely known, and still longer before he displayed any marked pride in his role as draftsman. One is tempted to ascribe this to wounded pride over congressional tinkering, but, in truth, Jefferson had not wanted to serve on the drafting committee. The Virginia convention was in the process of adopting a state constitution that summer, and that project seemed more important to Jefferson. The establishment of new governments in America, founded on principles of justice, reason, and humanity, was the truly important work of the Revolution.

Jefferson chafed at his enforced stay in Philadelphia, but he was determined to contribute to the framing of the Virginia government. While the convention labored away in the sticky heat of a Williamsburg summer, Jefferson drafted a model of his own, which he sent to Williamsburg via his old friend and mentor, George Wythe. Jefferson's draft was not a radical document, for he retained many of the features of Virginia's colonial regime. The most dramatic feature of it was a provision for universal manhood suffrage. Voting in the eighteenth century was considered a privilege, not a right. Every colony conditioned voting and officeholding on the possession of property on the theory that only the propertied, who had something to lose, would vote responsibly. Jefferson could not quite abandon this notion, or perhaps he recognized that his countrymen were not prepared to abandon it. He proposed instead to give every white adult male a fifty-acre freehold (that is, a plot of land held in unencumbered ownership), which, in turn, would be sufficient to meet the property requirement for voting and officeholding. Nevertheless, there were limits to his democratic instincts. His draft would have enfranchised men only. Jefferson, as most men of his time, considered women the weaker sex in both body and mind and thus unfit for a political role. While serving in France after the Revolution, he openly criticized the influence of women in French politics.

In other respects the draft constitution reflected his debt to the Whig historians who filled the shelves of his library. He consciously hoped to "re-establish such antient principles as are friendly to the rights of the people." Adopting the Whig preference for annual parliaments, Jefferson proposed annual elections for both houses of the Virginia legislature. He also wanted the governor elected annually and be ineligible for re-election for a period of five years. Although the executive would have been vested with most of the powers formerly held by the colonial governors, Jefferson would have denied him the power to veto legislation. Jefferson also prohibited standing armies in time of peace, relying instead on citizen-soldiers, a concept which, in Whig theory, originated with the Anglo-Saxons.

The convention received Jefferson's draft toward the end of its session. The delegates had already approved a document that solidified the position of the Tidewater gentry and made the legislature, still a gentlemen's club, the centerpiece of the government. They adopted Jefferson's preamble, which contained the now-familiar indictment of the king, and they ignored the rest. As a result, Jefferson became a severe critic of Virginia's constitution, and he conducted a lifelong crusade to change it. He failed at every turn. The constitution of 1776 remained virtually untouched until 1829, three years after his death.

WHEN THE VIRGINIA CONSTITUTIONAL CONVENTION reconstituted itself as the House of Delegates of the new state government in October 1776, Jefferson, having recovered from his illness, took his seat. The political creed that he brought to the assembly was the simple rationalism of the Declaration of Independence. But, unlike some of the European rationalists, Jefferson had no rage against the past. Nor, for that matter, did he have a Platonic blueprint for a perfect society. He was attached to the Virginia of his birth; he wished only to eliminate its abuses—the relics of feudalism, the privileges accorded the few, its massive popular ignorance, its religious establishment, and its dependence on slavery.

Patrick Henry had been elected governor, and Jefferson quickly filled the leadership vacuum in the assembly. His style differed markedly from that of Henry, however. Jefferson eschewed Henry's oratorical bombast; he was looked to instead because he had an agenda, a plan for improving Virginia society. He soon discovered an ally in James Madison, a new delegate from Orange County, just north of Jefferson's Albemarle in the Virginia Piedmont. A diminutive and quiet man of twenty-five years, Madison evinced a breadth of reading and a depth of wisdom that Jefferson would find ever useful in a lifelong collaboration. Madison had been educated at the College of New Jersey, in Princeton, whose Scottish president had imbued him with the political and religious thought of the Enlightenment. He made his mark as a reformer during Virginia's constitutional convention when he proposed an amendment to the Declaration of Rights favoring religious freedom. The Church of England (Episcopal in post-Revolutionary America) was established by law in colonial Virginia, as it was in the mother country. While other churches were tolerated, public taxes and other support went to the official church. Jefferson and Madison felt that the connection between church and state was an affront to intellectual freedom and a relic of Old World corruption, since crown and church had been partners in tyranny for centuries.

On October 12 the House gave Jefferson leave to draft a bill for the general revision of the laws. The bill passed two weeks later, and the House named a committee of five, chaired by Jefferson to carry out the work. The resulting legislation bore his stamp. The committee did not discard the body of colonial law; instead it streamlined it by discarding what was obsolete and useless. It also acted on the principle that the law should be reasonable and comprehensible, as well as humane. The revision of the law code took the committee almost three years; it finally issued its report in June 1779. In later years Jefferson bracketed legal reform with two other measures that he drafted during his legislative service, freedom of religion and educational reform, and viewed the whole "as forming a system by which every fiber would be eradicated of ancient or feudal aristocracy; and a foundation laid for government truly republican."

Unfortunately, Jefferson did not remain in the assembly long enough to steer his "system" through the legislative labyrinth. Not long after his report was published he moved on to the governorship, to Congress, and then to diplomatic service abroad. The many bills he had drafted in those three and a half years would be guided through the assembly by Madison. The report itself was never acted on as a unit; instead it became, as Madison expressed it, "a mine of legislative wealth" that occupied much of the assembly's time for more than a decade.

Jefferson's first bill, abolishing entail (feudal limitations on land inheritance), passed the assembly in November 1776. A related measure, abolishing primogeniture (inheritance by the eldest son when a person died without a will), was finally adopted on Madison's motion in 1785. Together with the abolition of quitrents, these measures eliminated the relics of feudalism from Virginia's land system and ensured that freeholds would be the prevailing land tenure thereafter in Virginia. Jefferson thought he was striking a blow against aristocracy. In a sense he was, but in freeing the economy of Virginia from the control of an entrenched aristocracy, he was also laying the foundation for free enterprise capitalism.

Jefferson sought to make the new state's criminal code more humane by reducing the number of crimes punishable by death to two—murder and treason. Jefferson was apparently unaware of the concept, being discussed among Enlightened men in Europe, of reforming wrongdoers by incarcerating them. He proposed instead to employ criminals on public works, in mines, roads, and shipyards, shaving their heads and dressing them in uniforms to discourage efforts to escape. Madison brought the bill enacting these reforms before the House in 1786, but it went down to defeat. Madison thought a "rage against horse stealing" responsible. That was an especially nefarious crime among Virginians and had been a capital offense since the middle of the century. However, a decade later the assembly enacted into law most of the features of Jefferson's bill.

Freedom of religion was the next item on Jefferson's agenda. Virginia's Declaration of Rights committed the new state to the idea that "all men are equally entitled to the free exercise of religion." However, this promise of toleration did not affect the fact that public taxes were used for the support of the Anglican establishment. Jefferson's conviction that church and state must be kept separate was founded on reason. The question of what is truth, he felt, must be submitted to the free marketplace of ideas; it could not be determined by the state and imposed by coercion. "It is error alone which needs the support of government," he declared. "Truth can stand by itself."

Jefferson's reasoning ran counter to the idea, endorsed by both Patrick Henry and Richard Henry Lee, that religious faith was essential to morality, and public support for religion was necessary for the survival of the republic. Fortunately for Jefferson, however, disestablishment appealed to Baptists and Presbyterians, who objected to paying taxes for the support of the Episcopal church. The Lee–Henry forces tried to counter this by introducing a bill for a general assessment on behalf of religion, to be distributed to the various churches at the designation of the taxpayers.

Jefferson drafted his Statute for Religious Freedom in 1779. The assembly terminated the official support for the Anglican church in that year, but it was not yet ready for Jefferson's concept of the total freedom to believe or, equally controversial, the freedom not to believe. The statute, which Jefferson later *xx ℋ. 90 a. 84*

A BILL for establishing RELIGIOUS FREEDOM, printed for the consideration of the PEOPLE.

WELL aware that the opinions and belief of men depend not on their own will, but follow involuntarily the evidence proposed to their minds, that Almighty God hath created the mind free, and manifested his Supreme will that free it shall remain, by making it altogether insusceptible of restraint: That all attempts to influence it by temporal punishments or burthens, or by civil incapacitations, tend only to beget habits of hypocrisy and meanness, and are a departure from the plan of the holy author of our religion, who being Lord both of body and mind, yet chose not to propagate it by coercions on either, as was in his Almighty power to do, but to extend it by its influence on reason alone: That the impious presumption of legislators and rulers, civil as well as ecclesiastical, who, being themselves but fallible and uninspired men, have assumed dominion over the faith of others, setting up their own opinions and modes of thinking, as the only true and infallible, and as such, endeavouring to impose them on others, hath established and maintained false religions over the greatest part of the world, and through all time: That to compel a man to furnish contributions of money for the propagation of opinions which he disbelieves and abhors, is sinful and tyrannical: That even the forcing him to support this or that teacher of his own religious persuasion, is depriving him of the comfortable liberty of giving his contributions to the particular pastor whose morals he would make his pattern, and whose powers he feels most persuasive to righteousness, and is withdrawing from the Ministry those temporal rewards which, proceeding from an approbation of their personal conduct, are an additional incitement to earnest and unremitting labour for the instruction of mankind: That our civil rights have no dependance on our religious opinions, any more than our opinions in physicks or geometry: That therefore the proscribing any citizen as unworthy the publick confidence, by laying upon him an incapacity of being called to offices of trust and emolument, unless he profess or renounce this or that religious opinion, is depriving him injuriously of those privileges and advantages to which, in common with his fellow citizens he has a natural right: That it tends also to corrupt the principles of that very religion it is meant to encourage, by bribing with a monopoly of wordly honours and emoluments, those who will externally profess and conform to it: That though indeed these are criminal who do not withstand such temptation, yet neither are those innocent who lay the bait in their way; That the opinions of men are not the object of civil government, nor under its jurisdiction: That to suffer the civil Magistrate to intrude his powers into the field of opinion, and to restrain the profession or propagation of principles on supposition of their ill tendency, is a dangerous fallacy, which at once destroys all religious liberty; because he being of course Judge of that tendency will make his own opinions the rule of judgment, and approve or condemn the sentiments of others only as they shall square with, or differ from his own: That it is time enough for the rightful purposes of civil government for its officers to interfere when principles break out into overt acts against peace and good order: And finally, that truth is great and will prevail if left to herself; that she is the proper and sufficient antagonist to errour, and has nothing to fear from the conflict, unless by human interposition, disarmed of her natural weapons, free argument and debate; errours ceasing to be dangerous when it is permitted freely to contradict them.

WE the General Assembly of *Virginia* do enact, that no man shall be compelled to frequent or support any religous Worship place or Ministry whatsoever, nor shall be enforced, restrained, molested, or burthened in his body or goods, nor shall otherwise suffer on account of his religious opinions or belief, but that all men shall be free to profess, and by argument to maintain their opinions in matters of religion, and that the same shall in no wise diminish, enlarge, or affect their civil capacities.

AND though we well know that this Assembly, elected by the people for the ordinary purposes of legislation only, have no power to restrain the acts of succeeding Assemblies, constituted with powers equal to our own, and that therefore to declare this act irrevocable would be of no effect in law; yet we are free to declare, and do declare, that the rights hereby asserted are of the natural rights of mankind, and that if any act shall be hereafter passed to repeal the present, or to narrow its operation, such act will be an infringement of natural right.

c

Jefferson was extremely proud of his efforts to insure religious freedom in Virginia. This is the earliest printed text of the Bill for the Establishment of Religious Freedom.

regarded as one of the three supreme achievements of his life, was finally steered through the assembly by Madison in 1786.

Jefferson's proposals on education and slavery met with less success. Educational reform was tied to the eighteenth-century concept of republican virtue. Because in a republic government rested on the will of the people, it would not long survive republican and free unless the people were adequately informed and instructed. The best way to impart virtue, he felt, was to acquaint people with a reliable understanding of the past. After studying the experiences of the Greeks, Romans, and the English, Virginians would be better equipped "to know ambition under all its shapes, and [be] prompt to exert their natural powers to defeat its purposes." Jefferson therefore concluded that education was too important to be left to chance or wealth, which was much the same thing. It was one of the primary functions of republican government.

In 1778 he brought before the House a Bill for the More General Diffusion of Knowledge. He projected three distinct levels of education: elementary, middle, and higher. At the elementary level each county would be divided into wards, each of a size suitable for a school. All free children, male and female (presumably including free blacks), would be educated at governmental expense for three years; they could stay in school longer at the expense of their parents. At that level, in addition to reading, writing, and arithmetic, children would receive instruction in the rights and duties of citizens. The moral lessons in this regard, however, were to be drawn from history, not the Bible.

The government also financed the training at the second level, except for students "in easy circumstances," who would be charged tuition and board. Democratic though his inclinations were, Jefferson could not temperamentally escape Virginia's hierarchical social system. Under his plan one-third of the students in the secondary schools would be eliminated after the first year, except for the best scholar in each of the district schools. By this method, Jefferson wrote, "twenty of the best geniuses will be raked from the rubbish annually, and be instructed, at the public expense, so far as grammar schools go." Ten of these twenty would be allowed to attend the College of William and Mary, which stood at the apex of Jefferson's educational pyramid. He drafted a companion bill to convert the College from an Anglican-controlled institution into a state university offering instruction in all branches of knowledge.

The availability of a state institution of higher learning, Jefferson hoped, would discourage Virginia youth from studying abroad. He agreed with the English Country writer James Burgh that the English universities Oxford and Cambridge were "little better than seminaries of vice." European education, Jefferson felt, instilled in American youths "a fondness for European luxury and dissipation," a contempt for the simplicity of their own country, and "a passion for whores, destructive of health." And most menacing of all was the likelihood of developing "a partiality for aristocracy or monarchy."

Nothing came of Jefferson's plan; it was far too radical for the assembly. Indeed, the idea of tax-supported public education did not become current in the North until the 1830s, and southern states did not embrace the idea until after the Civil War. As governor, however, he was able to make some changes at William and Mary. He replaced professorships in divinity, oriental languages, Greek, and Latin with professorships in law and government, anatomy and medicine, and modern languages. These changes foretold the revolutionary changes in university curriculum that he would institute in founding the University of Virginia thirty-seven years later.

The fate of Jefferson's efforts to modify the institution of slavery revealed the limits of revolutionary social reform, as well as the limits of Jefferson's own idealism. His model draft for the Virginia constitution prohibited the holding in slavery of any person who henceforth entered the state, which presumably applied to imports from other states as well as from Africa. This echoed his denunciation of slavery in the Declaration of Independence, a blend of humanitarianism and a wish to diversify Virginia's economy. Although the legislature was unwilling to go that far, in 1778 it did slam the door on further imports from Africa. Jefferson later claimed authorship of this measure, and that seems likely. In its original form the bill sought to encourage private manumission of slaves, but that provision was deleted by the assembly before passage. After the Revolution Jefferson turned his attention to the problem of preventing the spread of slavery into the West. However, he eventually compromised even that modest approach, concluding that the diffusion of slavery might ameliorate the living conditions of the slaves. To the end of his life Jefferson opposed slavery in principle, but in practice he did little to alter or eliminate the "peculiar institution."

JEFFERSON TOOK HIS SEAT IN THE House of Delegates when its session opened in May 1779 and soon found himself nominated for governor. Given the prominent role he had played in the House and his prior service in Congress, his elevation to governor was both logical and deserved. He did not seek the office, but neither did he attempt to dissuade the friends who supported him. "In a virtuous government, and more especially in times like these," he explained to a friend, "public offices are, what they should be, burthens to those appointed to them which it would be wrong to decline, though foreseen to bring with them intense labor and great private loss." He thus accepted the office out of a sense of duty, with a realization that a wartime executive faces uncommon burdens. His misgivings proved out. He served a tempestuous two years and left the office in utter humiliation.

Most Americans looked askance at executive power. In most colonies the governor had represented royal authority; his relationship with the people and their elected representatives was, more often than not, one of confrontation. Nearly every state constitution delegated few powers to the governor, making the office secondary to the legislature, and Virginia was no exception. Providing for the election of the governor by the assembly rendered him subject to that body and prevented him from developing a popular electoral base. In addition, the state constitution provided for one-year terms, which meant that the governor received an annual review in the fickle and querulous House of Delegates. In addition, Virginia's governor was required to work closely with the Council of State. He could not make appointments or call out the militia without the consent of the eight-man Council. Fortunately for Jefferson, James Madison

Long after Jefferson's tenure as governor Richmond retained its classical character. In this 1797 sketch Jefferson's Grecian state house looms over the village that became the state capital during the Revolution. *View of Richmond from Bushrod Washington's Island* in the James River, watercolor by Benjamin H. Latrobe. *Courtesy of the Maryland Historical Society, Baltimore.*

served on the Council during Jefferson's term as governor, and this greatly facilitated his relations with that body. Indeed, the life-long collaboration of Jefferson and Madison began in this period. Worst of all, the assembly kept control of military and commercial affairs through a board of war and a board of trade, which produced much confusion and delay in decision-making.

Adding to the confusion at the inception of Jefferson's term was the move of the capital from Williamsburg to Richmond. Jefferson himself had initiated the idea two years earlier, arguing that Richmond was more centrally located and more easily defended. The assembly held up the move until after it elected him governor. Jefferson occupied the governor's palace in Williamsburg during his first year in office. He then accompanied the assembly and the public records when the government officially moved to Richmond the following April. Only thirty-five years old, Richmond was a sleepy village of 1,800 inhabitants situated at the falls of the James River, about eighty miles west of Williamsburg. Jefferson leased one of the few houses in town that could lay claim to any sort of elegance—a brick house with garden on Shockoe Hill. There he settled with his family, slaves, and forty-nine boxes of books and furniture on a cold day in April 1780.

The war entered a new and, for Virginia, ominous phase at the end of 1778 when Sir Henry Clinton, commander-in-chief of the British armies, decided to abandon the effort to restore the northern states to the empire and to concentrate on the recovery of the staple-producing states in the South. He personally led a force that seized Savannah in December 1778 and Augusta a month later. Virginia felt the impact of the new British strategy on May 10, 1779, when a British fleet sailed into Hampton Roads (at the mouth of the James River) and landed 1,800 troops. The British seized Portsmouth and plundered the surrounding countryside for two weeks before setting sail for New York.

The raid revealed how defenseless Virginia was. Chesapeake Bay with its many deep estuaries gave a seaborne enemy easy access to the very heart of the state. Virginia had no navy, and her regular troops were serving with Washington in New York. Defense of the state thus rested on the militia, citizen soldiers who dropped their plows and picked up their muskets at the call of the governor. Or at least that was how the militia was supposed to function. In practice only frontiersmen were well armed, and most of these were occupied in the defense of Kentucky against Indians. Few of the farmers in eastern Virginia had firearms, and the state's own arsenal had long since been emptied in response to General Washington's calls for help. Jefferson nevertheless realized that Virginia's security depended on the outcome of the fighting in South Carolina. As the British probed toward Charleston in the spring of 1779, he sent every army recruit he could find to the southward, along with whatever arms and ammunition were left in the state.

Money was at the root of Virginia's evils. Currency had

always been in short supply, and tax evasion was widespread. Half the counties failed to meet their tax obligations in 1779. In May the legislature allowed taxes to be paid in commodities, such as tobacco and deerskins, but that created new problems of collection and transportation. From the beginning the assembly had financed the war by issuing paper money, but its value depreciated rapidly because there was no gold or silver in the treasury to support it. Currency depreciation created disaffection in the army and encouraged speculation in the civilian economy. But the legislature had no choice but to keep the presses turning. "The inundation of paper money appears to have overflowed virtue," one Virginian fretted in June 1779, "and I fear will bury the liberty of America in the same grave."

Jefferson had long advocated economic diversity for Virginia, and as governor he thought that the development of manufactures would further the war effort and restore public solvency. Independence did encourage some entrepreneurs to undertake the weaving of cloth, the tanning of leather, and the manufacture of gunpowder. Jefferson took a keen interest in these enterprises and even persuaded the assembly to authorize construction of a public arms factory on the James River. The project failed to meet Jefferson's expectations in part because there were few skilled artisans in Virginia, and the French government refused to allow its munitions workers to emigrate. Virginia thus remained dependent on outside sources for firearms and many other manufactures as well.

After a year of maneuvering in the swampy low country of South Carolina General Clinton's army attacked Charleston in the spring of 1780. The army defending the city, 5,000 strong, surrendered on May 12. Virginia lost its entire Continental line in the defeat, and the state's morale plummeted to a new low. General Clinton returned to New York, leaving his trusted lieutenant, Charles Lord Cornwallis, to secure South Carolina. Before the end of May Cornwallis crossed the Santee River with an army of 4,000, augmented daily by Loyalist recruits. North Carolina lay virtually helpless in his path.

Before Charleston fell, General Washington had dispatched

the Maryland and Delaware Continentals, some of the finest troops in his army, to the southern theater. Luckily, these had been detained in Virginia by a lack of wagons, and they became the core of a new army for the defense of the South. Jefferson called out the Virginia militia, and by mid-summer he was able to inform Washington that a southern army numbering 10,000 was in place. Unfortunately, most of it consisted of untrained and poorly armed North Carolina and Virginia farmers. To head this force Congress chose General Horatio Gates, victor over the British at Saratoga. Gates hastened to South Carolina, met Cornwallis at Camden in August, and saw his citizen soldiers melt in the face of British bayonets. Gates himself fled the battlefield along with the militia, leaving the Continentals to conduct a courageous rear-guard action.

Jefferson's response to this disaster was to redouble his efforts to prepare Virginia for war. He issued a new call for 2,500 militia, and he ordered his county lieutenants (militia commanders) to arrest all deserters, try them by court marital, and sentence them to eight months service in the regular army. He told Washington that Virginia would be able to defend itself, but the British belied this optimistic forecast by once again landing an amphibious force at the mouth of the James. Although Virginia's Tidewater lay at their mercy, the British showed no appetite for conquest and contented themselves with the occupation of Portsmouth. Jefferson soon realized that the British purpose was to maintain a base in Virginia that would distract the Virginians and disrupt the flow of supplies into the Carolinas. Before he could do much the British force abruptly departed, having been summoned to Charleston by Cornwallis, a segment of whose army had been defeated at King's Mountain.

After the disaster at Camden, Congress allowed Washington to choose a new commander in the South. Washington selected Nathanael Greene, the best tactician among his lieutenants. Greene arrived in Richmond in November, accompanied by "Baron" Friedrich William Augustus von Steuben, the Prussian volunteer who had shaped Washington's army into European-style professionals at Valley Forge. Greene placed von Steuben in command of Virginia, charged with forwarding the reinforcements of men and supplies to the Southern Army. During the winter of 1780–1781 von Steuben stripped Virginia of regular soldiers, forwarding them to Greene, and, on a theory that no enemy was in sight, he induced Jefferson to send the militia home.

The folly of von Steuben's actions became clear on a mild Sunday morning, the last day of the year, when twenty-seven sail were spotted rounding Cape Charles and entering Chesapeake Bay. Two days passed before the force was identified as British, but Jefferson then acted quickly. On January 2 he summoned the Council and called 4,600 militia into the field. The traitor Benedict Arnold was in command of the British force. Demonstrating the energy that had made him a hero in the Saratoga campaign, prior to his treason, Arnold sailed straight up the James and landed 1,500 men at Westover, the Byrd plantation a few miles below Richmond. The militia were just beginning to assemble, and only 200 were available to defend the town. Jefferson sent his family up-river to the Randolph plantation at Tuckahoe, and he left town alone on horseback. He spent the next few days riding the countryside, trying to locate von Steuben and coordinate a defense. In the saddle for thirty-six hours without rest, he rode one horse to death and had to buy another from a farmer. From Manchester, across the James River, Jefferson watched in helpless frustration as Arnold set fire to the public buildings and tobacco warehouses. Arnold lacked the men to hold Richmond, and after a few days he evacuated the town. His mission had been the same as that of the earlier British invasion—disrupt Greene's supply line and damage Virginia morale. Having succeeded in both, he retired to Portsmouth to await the arrival of Cornwallis in Virginia.

In February 1781 Washington sent a new force of 1,200 regulars to Virginia under the command of the French volunteer, Marquis de Lafayette. Jefferson responded with a call for 3,000 militia to give Lafayette the strength to push Arnold out of Portsmouth. Before Lafayette could move, Cornwallis, having fought Greene to a draw at Guilford Court House, North Carolina, in March, invaded Virginia. Simultaneously, on April 18, a new amphibious force under General William Phillips sailed into the James River. Instead of proceeding to Richmond, he raided Williamsburg, which gave Jefferson time to move the government and its records westward. The assembly convened in Charlottesville in May.

On May 20 Cornwallis linked up with Phillips at Petersburg. He chased Lafayette out of Richmond and sent a detachment of rangers to Charlottesville to capture the assembly and the governor. Warned by an alert militiaman, Jack Jouett, who spotted the rangers on the road to Charlottesville, the assembly hastily adjourned and fled across the Blue Ridge to Staunton. Jouett also stopped at Monticello to warn Jefferson of the danger. The governor sent his family to a neighboring plantation and rode to Carter's Mountain, a nearby hill, from whence he could watch the British in Charlottesville through his telescope. The raiders, led by Lieutenant Colonel Banastre Tarleton, arrived at Monticello, found no one but slaves, and left without doing any damage. Cornwallis set up headquarters for a time at Elk Hill, another of Jefferson's plantations. His men did considerable damage there, burning barns and fences for firewood and slaughtering cattle and sheep. Cornwallis took 27 slaves with him when he departed. Jefferson conceded that Cornwallis would have "done right" if his object was to give the slaves their freedom. However, he later learned that the real outcome "was to consign them to inevitable death from the small pox and putrid fever then raging in his camp." That indeed was the fate of most of them; Jefferson recaptured only five when Cornwallis surrendered.

Jefferson was less of a prize for Cornwallis to capture for he was by then a private citizen, his term as governor having expired on June 2. It was the worst possible time for him to leave office. Virginia's pride had been shattered, Jefferson had not yet been replaced as governor, and the legislature was looking for a scapegoat. Washington had dispatched fresh troops—the Pennsylvania line under General Anthony Wayne—to reinforce Lafayette. In September Washington himself would appear in Virginia, along with a French naval squadron. Together Washington and the French would trap Cornwallis at the seaside village of Yorktown, forcing a surrender that ended the fighting in the Revolution. Because of all his labor in the cause, Jefferson certainly deserved to share in the glory of this victory, but it was not to be. Instead he had to suffer legislative censorship for the humiliation visited upon Virginia in Cornwallis's campaign.

The legislature in June discussed a proposal to name a dictator to straighten out Virginia's government. Washington's name was mentioned at the time, but Jefferson suspected that Patrick Henry was behind the move. Jefferson and Henry had parted ways politically after the Revolution began. Essentially a conservative on social issues, Henry had fought every feature of Jefferson's legislative reforms. When Jefferson replaced Henry in the governor's chair, Henry became his leading critic in the assembly. The proposal for a dictator failed, and Jefferson, when he learned of the debate from an eyewitness, soundly denounced the idea. The goal of the Revolution, he wrote, was liberty; its whole ideology would be subverted if it yielded to despotism. "The very thought alone was treason against the people."

The House of Delegates then turned on Jefferson himself, passing a resolution setting up an inquiry into the conduct of the executive during the crisis. Jefferson thought that this move too was guided by the hand of Patrick Henry. The accusations against the executive, that is, both Governor and Council, all related to Arnold's invasion of the previous winter. No investigation materialized, and the following winter the House and Senate agreed on a resolution affirming "the high opinion which they entertain of Mr. Jefferson's Ability, Rectitude, and Integrity as chief Magistrate of this Commonwealth, and mean by thus publicly avowing their opinion, to obviate and remove all unmerited Censure." Unfortunately, the censure implicit in the original motion for an investigation could not be removed. It pursued him the rest of his life and into the history books. His final days as governor were the nadir of his public career.

Chapter Three

———————————○———————————

Freedom's Minister

THE MOMENT THAT THE ASSEMBLY exonerated him Jefferson departed for Monticello, informing friends that he was determined never to leave it. In addition to his sense of having been wronged, love and duty drove him home. Martha was again with child, their sixth, and every previous pregnancy had been a crisis because of her poor health. The medical information is scant, but her slow yet visible decline over many years suggests the possibility of a blood disorder, possibly anemia. Jefferson knew only that his role, for the moment, was that of loving companion and nursemaid.

He tried at first to resume his scholarly interests. Six months earlier, following his escape from Tarleton's raiders, Jefferson had begun a lengthy description of his homeland that would ultimately be published as *Notes on Virginia*. He did it in part as an escape from his accumulating miseries—the British invasion, the assembly's investigation, Martha's ill health, and, finally, a fall from his horse that left him with a broken wrist and housebound for six weeks. Physically impaired, he had kept his mind active by responding to a series of 23 questions about Virginia sent to him by a member of the French legation in Philadelphia. He began then to answer the questions in some detail, and he continued the project after returning to Monticello in December 1781. The answers would be published in 1784 as a 200-page book, and it established Jefferson's reputation in America and in Europe as a pioneer scientist, historian, and geographer. It was a signal accomplishment for a man who had been immersed in politics for more than a decade, and who was at the time managing the economy of half a dozen plantations, supervising the construction of a country squire's mansion on a mountaintop, and caring for an ailing wife.

The *Notes on Virginia*, the first scientific survey of a portion of North America, was a compilation of observations that Jefferson had made in his travels and notes he had taken on his casual reading. The work revealed the breadth and depth of his lifelong pursuit of knowledge. With remarkable accuracy he described Virginia's geology, natural history, fauna, flora, human population, agriculture, manufacturing, and government. The *Notes* is a mine of information for scholars today, as well as a standing reminder of what has been lost since Jefferson's day. In one of his many lyrical passages Jefferson described the Ohio as "the most beautiful river on earth; its current gentle, waters clear and bosom smooth and unbroken."

In the section on manufactures Jefferson digressed into an encomium on agriculture and the virtues of rural life. It was one of the most famous passages in the book and one that would haunt his political ideology all his life:

> Those who labour in the earth are the chosen people of God, if ever he had a chosen people, whose breasts he has made a peculiar deposit for substantial and genuine virtue. . . . While we have land to labour then, let us never wish to see our citizens occupied at a work bench, or twirling a distaff. Carpenters, masons, smiths are wanting in husbandry: but, for the general operations of manufacture, let our workshops remain in Europe. . . . The mobs of great cities add just so much to the support of pure government, as sores do to the strength of the human body. It is the manners and spirit of a people which preserve a republic in vigour.

As we have seen, Jefferson was not averse to commerce; indeed, he had striven mightily to secure Virginia's commercial independence. And he favored manufactures, so long as they were located in the countryside and interwoven with the needs of agriculture. His aversion to cities—an aversion shared by middle-class "radicals" in Britain—as that they were home to courts, officeholders, pensioners, retainers, the idle (both rich and poor), luxury, and waste. The countryside he associated with individualism, hard work, honesty, and the spirit of enterprise.

His poetic descriptions of the American landscape revealed his pride in his native country, as well as a desire to promote its blessings before an international audience. It was in this spirit that he digressed from a discussion of Virginia's plants and animals to pick a quarrel with the leading naturalist of Europe, Comte Georges de Buffon. One of several French Encyclopedists who, impelled by the Enlightenment, sought to codify all of human knowledge, Buffon had been working for forty years on his *Histoire Naturale* (ultimately published in 44 quarto volumes). Not content with the mere collection of data, Buffon had inserted some theories of his own, which had wide credence in Europe. Among these was the notion that because of the damp, cold climate and "niggardly sky," everything in America degenerated, so that both animals and humans were punier in size and vitality (and presumably in intelligence) than their counterparts in Europe. As an example—and it was a clue to his scientific method—Buffon cited male Indians, who had neither beards nor any visible body hair. Jefferson demolished this thesis by carefully comparing the largest known weights of animals found on both continents. He pointed out that the biggest American cow was almost 2,000 pounds heftier than its European cousin. (His argument would have been even more conclusive if he had known that cows were not native to America, but had been introduced from Europe.) Nor would he leave unanswered Buffon's aspersions on the American Indian. In an eloquent defense of the Native American, Jefferson noted that he was brave enough to "defend himself against a host of enemies," yet "affectionate to his children," and in friendship "strong and faithful to the utmost extremity." To prove that an Indian's "vivacity and activity of mind was fully equal to a white man," Jefferson quoted the speech of Logan, a Mingo leader who defiantly declared that he had gone to war because treacherous whites had murdered his family. With perhaps pardonable exaggeration, Jefferson compared Chief Logan's speech with the greatest orations of history.

When he reached the subject of African Americans, Jefferson launched into a dispassionate, scientific discussion of racial characteristics. As a result of his own observations, he had some doubts as to whether blacks were equal in intelligence to whites, but he admitted that he had been able to study them only in the degraded condition of slavery. Turning to slavery, he shed his objectivity and drew a devastating picture of the effects of the institution on both blacks and whites. "The whole commerce between master and slave," he wrote, "is a perpetual exercise of the most boisterous passions, the most unremitting despotism on the one part, and degrading submissions on the other." Slavery made white men lazy and, worse still, undermined their respect for human rights and freedom. He had argued in the Declaration of Independence that the unalienable rights of man were derived from God. He contended now that they could not be violated but by incurring His wrath. "Indeed I tremble for my country when I reflect that god is just; that his justice cannot sleep forever."

Early in the spring of 1782 one of the commanders of the French army at Yorktown, Major General Marquis de Chastellux, visited Monticello and found Jefferson still working on the book. It was the first time the two had met, although they had corresponded during the fighting. "I found his first appearance serious, nay even cold," Chastellux confided to his diary. "But before I had been two hours with him, we were as intimate as if we had passed our whole lives together." Everyone who became close to Jefferson had this same experience. Once Jefferson found in another a kindred spirit, he became as intimate and personable as if the friend were family. They quickly discovered a mutual love for music and poetry, and the four days that Chastellux spent at Monticello passed, he said, "like so many minutes."

When Chastellux departed, Jefferson persuaded him to ride eighty miles farther south in Virginia to see the Natural Bridge, which Jefferson always contended was one of the great natural wonders of the world. Jefferson accompanied the Frenchman only to the ford of the Mechum River, sixteen miles from Monticello because Martha was momentarily expected to give birth. And she did, a few days later. It was a girl, whom they named Lucy Elizabeth, after an infant they had lost two years earlier during the trying days in Richmond.

Martha did not rally from the birth; instead she slowly wasted away for the next four months while Jefferson watched helplessly in torment of soul. Jefferson scarcely left her bedside during all that time, though he had nursing help from both his own sister, Mrs. Dabney Carr, and Martha's sister, Elizabeth Eppes. When on the sixth of September 1782, Martha sank into a coma and her breathing became labored, Jefferson blacked out and had to be dragged from the room by his female helpers. The scene was witnessed by Jefferson's daughter Martha, age ten. Some fifty years later, Martha wrote, "The violence of his emotion . . . to this day I do not trust myself to describe."

Jefferson buried himself in his library for three weeks, and for weeks after that he could do nothing but ride aimlessly around the countryside. He might have moldered at Monticello forever, an eccentric recluse driven to the depths by grief and humiliation, but he was rescued by an old political ally, James Madison. The little man with an expansive mind and a warm heart was then serving in the Confederation Congress (where, incidentally, he was forming bonds with Alexander Hamilton of New York and James Wilson of Pennsylvania, two statesmen who would help immensely in the movement to reform the government and draft a federal Constitution). Having heard tales of Jefferson's extraordinary grief, Madison presented a motion that he be named a commissioner to join the American envoys in Paris who were negotiating an end to war. Congress unanimously agreed, and Jefferson accepted with alacrity. Monticello, for the moment, had lost its charm, and he needed a new channel for his energies.

Before he could sail, news arrived of the signing, in November 1782, of preliminary articles of peace between the United States and Britain, and Congress withdrew its commission. At that point the Virginia assembly stepped in and elected him a delegate to the Confederation Congress, directing him to present himself to that body on the first of November 1783. Jefferson spent the summer cataloguing his library of 2,640 books and supervising the education of eleven-year-old Martha. It was extremely important that she get good home instruction, he explained to a French friend, because schools in Virginia were poor and "the chance that in marriage she will draw a blockhead I calculate at about 14 to 1." (She eventually wed future governor of Virginia, Thomas Mann Randolph, Jr.) When Jefferson departed for Philadelphia in the fall, he took Martha with him.

Congress was no longer meeting in Philadelphia, having been chased out by mutinous soldiers demanding back pay. Jefferson finally caught up with it at Annapolis. He had missed nothing. Not until December 13 was Congress able to obtain a quorum of seven states, and this permitted it to take on only minor business since the approval of nine states was required under the Articles of Confederation for most important matters. The quality of Congress had deteriorated markedly since the days when Jefferson last served. The giants of '76 were either in retirement or in the service of their states. Even the monumental intellects that Madison had encountered in the previous session had departed. What remained was a collection of self-important nobodies, most of whom, Jefferson said later, were "afflicted with the morbid rage of debate."

In such a group Jefferson quickly emerged as a leader. In the course of the five-month session he wrote no fewer than thirty-one committee reports. Among these was a report on a monetary system for the new nation. Although some favored retaining the English system of pounds, shillings, and pence, Jefferson determined instead on a decimal system because it was easier and more rational. As a base, he selected the Spanish silver dollar or "piece of eight" because it was well known and had circulated for years in the colonies as a by-product of the trade with the Spanish Indies. Unfortunately, Jefferson left Congress before he could submit his plan in the form of a resolution. Friends kept it alive, however, and in 1785 Congress approved the scheme in principle. Implementation had to await the advent of the federal government and the work of Treasury Secretary Alexander Hamilton.

Jefferson's most important task during the session was drafting an ordinance of government for the Northwest Territory. Led by Virginia, which had ceded its claims to the territory north of the Ohio River in 1781, states with western land claims had ceded them to Congress. (Virginia retained control of Kentucky, which became a state in 1792; North Carolina did not relinquish its claims over Tennessee until 1789; and Georgia held a shaky claim to the area south of the Tennessee River until 1800.) By 1784, Congress possessed an empire of its own bounded by the Great Lakes, the Ohio River, and the Mississippi. Although it had not obtained title from the Native American tribes of the area, Congress planned to sell the land to thousands of settlers, using the proceeds to pay the nation's war debt. That, in turn, raised the problem of government, for it would have been imprudent to let the frontiersmen fend for themselves. Separatist movements were already brewing among the settlers of Kentucky, Tennessee, and Pennsylvania.

The only available model for the government of thinly inhabited territory was the great European empires, and there were many in Congress who wished to keep the West in a kind of colonial dependency. Jefferson, however, struck boldly in a new direction. His committee report set up the principle that western territories, when they reached a certain number of inhabitants, should be incorporated into the union on a par with the original thirteen states. He envisioned a relatively brief territorial stage, allowing them to become states when they obtained a mere twenty thousand inhabitants. Jefferson drew a rough map, laying out possible boundaries for fourteen new states in the Northwest, even supplying exotic names for some of them, such as Assenisipia, Metropotamia, Polypotamia, and Pelisipia. Under Jefferson's plan the West, which he anticipated would be populated by small, democratically minded property owners, would have soon become a major political force. He imposed only one requirement on the western states, that they be "republican" in form; decisions concerning qualifications for voting and officeholding he would leave to the westerners themselves. However, he added one other caveat. After the year 1800, Jefferson proposed, "neither slavery nor involuntary servitude" would be permitted in any of the western states. Having failed to eradicate slavery in his own state, Jefferson hoped at least to prevent the spread of it into the West.

When Jefferson's proposed ordinance reached the floor of Congress, southern delegates attacked the antislavery clause. To retain it required the affirmative vote of seven states. By then ten of the thirteen states had managed to send delegates. Six northern states voted to keep it; three southern states, including Virginia, to Jefferson's mortification, voted to delete it (Virginia's three-man delegation out-voted him two to one). The tenth state, New Jersey, had only one delegate in attendance because another was sick, and the rules of Congress required at least two delegates in order for a state to register a vote. Thus, the first assault on the nation's worst social cancer failed due to the illness of a single individual. Jefferson, still mindful of God's wrath, marveled: "And Heaven was silent in that awful moment!"

The Ordinance of 1784 itself failed to secure Congress' approval, in part because, under Jefferson's system, the West would have soon overwhelmed the seaboard states. Nevertheless, his concept of western statehood, as well as his restriction on slavery, would eventually triumph, when Congress again took up the subject of western governance in the Northwest Ordinance of 1787.

Although Congress rejected Jefferson's most cherished plans, it retained a high regard for him. Toward the end of the session in May 1784 it took up a proposal for increasing American representation abroad. John Adams and Benjamin Franklin were in Europe attempting to negotiate trade agreements on behalf of the new republic; Congress felt a southerner should be added to the team. In addition, a new minister to France would soon be needed, for the seventy-eight-year-old Franklin was begging to be relieved. The Paris embassy was a crucial post because France was America's only friend in Europe, and the two countries were still bound by Franklin's wartime alliance. The natural choice for the post was Jefferson. Thus, after three commissions that had proved to be false starts, Jefferson would at last see Europe, which he had longed to visit ever since his days as a student.

He eagerly seized the opportunity and quickly made arrangements. Albemarle neighbors would look after his estate. Seven-year-old Mary, or "Polly" as Jefferson was fond of calling her, and "Lu," as he called the infant Lucy Elizabeth, would remain with Aunt Elizabeth Eppes, where they had been since the death of his wife. Martha he would take with him. He made these arrangements in three days, and, without returning home, started north from Annapolis. He boarded a swift-sailing merchantman in Newport, Rhode Island, and landed in England nineteen days later. By August 6, 1784, he was in Paris where he rented a house on the Champs-Elysees and furnished it, so he complained to friends at home, with more elegance than he could afford. He put Martha in a convent school with a reputation for excellence and where the abbess was a "woman of the world," meaning that religion was not a stressed part of the curriculum. A year later Jefferson's diplomatic status changed when he replaced Franklin as U.S. minister to France, and John Adams journeyed to London to open diplomatic relations with the former mother country. Jefferson moved into a more sumptuous house on the left bank of the Seine, a few doors from the aristocratic Rochefoucauld family, who were enthusiastic lovers of America and the center of a group of enlightened *philosophes*.

His elegant surroundings and the excitement of life in Paris were not enough, however, to overcome his periodic fits of depression. In November 1785 he wrote a friend that he had "relapsed into the state of ill health in which you saw me in Annapolis, but more severe. I have had few hours wherein I could do anything." In January he was further devastated by news that little Lu had died—"a martyr to the complicated evils of teething, worms, and hooping cough." Of the six children that his wife had bore him, only two were left, Martha and Polly. The blow left him physically ill, given to recurrent migraines, and utterly despondent. John Adams's wife Abigail described him as "very week and feeble," and in March Jefferson told his Virginia friend James Monroe that he had been "confined the greater part" of the winter. His spirits lifted in the spring, nevertheless, and he began walking "six or eight miles a day." By summer he was in full vigor, and he began touring the French countryside, observing its inhabitants, and savoring French cuisine. He was so taken with French cooking that he paid several hundred dollars to bring one of his slaves, James Hemings, from Monticello to learn the chef's art from the *maitre* of his house in Paris.

With health restored, Jefferson began to take seriously his duties as minister to France. He had gone to Europe with an agenda of promoting worldwide freedom of trade. Whether or not he had read Adam Smith's celebrated *Wealth of Nations* at this point is uncertain, but he was certainly able to paraphrase the central concept of the new economics of *laissez faire*: "Instead of embarrassing commerce under piles of regulating laws, duties and prohibitions, could it be relieved from all its shackles in all parts of the world, could every country be employed in producing that which nature had best fitted it to produce, and each be free to exchange with others mutual surpluses for mutual wants, the greatest mass possible would then be produced of those things which contribute to human life and human happiness; the numbers of mankind would be increased, and their conditions bettered."

Jefferson early concluded that the best way to promote Franco-American trade was to increase French purchases of tobacco. Other American products would follow, and Americans would then be able to afford the purchase of French wines, silks, and oils. The British monopoly of American trade would be broken, and trade agreements with other countries might follow. Unfortunately, a well-entrenched remnant of French mercantilism, the Farmers-General, which had a monopoly on the import of tobacco into France, stood in the way of this vision. The Farmers-General, a company of wealthy merchants, collected customs duties on tobacco and other imports, and, after deducting a healthy sum for their services, the Farmers passed the remnant on to the coffers of the king. Jefferson tried to persuade the Comte de Vergennes, France's foreign minister, that the king would improve his revenues if he abolished the monopoly, collected the taxes himself, and lowered the duties to encourage imports. Vergennes agreed, but before an agreement could be reached Jefferson learned of another obstacle—Philadelphia merchant Robert Morris had negotiated a deal with the Farmers-General that gave him an exclusive three-year contract for the supply of American tobacco.

Working closely with Lafayette, Jefferson persuaded Vergennes to form a special committee to study means of promoting Franco-American commerce. The American Committee, as it came to be called, was unable to break the monopoly of the Farmers-General, but at a meeting in May 1786 it ordered the farm to purchase annually 12,000 to 15,000 hogsheads of American tobacco over and above the 20,000 that Morris had contracted to supply. Further, it agreed that when Morris's contract expired, no similar one was to be made. The committee's final report in October 1786 confirmed the arrangements on tobacco and reduced import duties on a large number of American products, from furs to ships. To Jefferson's dismay, the committee's recommendations were never fully implemented, but the principle of more open trade had been established.

In his last years in France Jefferson concentrated on introducing yet another raw product of American plantations, South Carolina rice. The obstacle here was not monopoly but ignorance. Rice was not a standard in French cuisine. However, he managed to persuade one of the liberal merchants with whom he had worked on the American Committee to accept some shipments from Charleston. The South Carolinians lost money at first, but by 1789 rice shipments were such that the South Carolina Agricultural Society honored Jefferson for the efforts he had made on the state's behalf.

In addition to his efforts to reach trade agreements with the French government, Jefferson actively promoted the blessings, natural and political, of his homeland. One of his first targets was the arrogant deprecator of America, Count Buffon. Jefferson had come to France prepared to resume his quarrel with the French naturalist. Before sailing he had purchased a panther skin, and he carried that to France as proof that the American animal was larger than its European relatives. Introduced to Buffon by Chastellux, Jefferson triumphantly unwrapped his skin. Confronted by visible proof, Buffon admitted that he was wrong. However, when Jefferson claimed that American deer and moose were larger than their Old World counterparts, Buffon scoffed. Determined to prove his point, Jefferson wrote to President John Sullivan of New Hampshire asking him to find a moose big enough to silence Buffon. Sullivan, who had been one of Washington's lieutenants in the Revolution, sent an army of hunters into the woods, and they succeeded in killing a giant. The animal was so big that the governor had to have a road cut into the woods so the monster could be hauled out by sleigh. Sullivan had it stuffed and mounted and shipped to Jefferson. It arrived in rather sad condition; most of the hair had fallen off. However, he sent it on to the opinionated Frenchman and received the satisfaction of a promise that Buffon would revise his theories of North American animals in the next volume of his *Histoire Naturale*. Unfortunately, the Frenchman died a few months later, and Jefferson never obtained a public apology.

Although he seemed to see himself as a one-man chamber of commerce, Jefferson was not blinded by pride of country. He saw rather that his young nation might benefit immensely by adopting European advances in agriculture and industry. Everywhere he traveled he collected seeds and shoots, which he sent to friends in America for experimental planting—grape vines from France, rice and beans from Italy. To George Washington, famed as an experimental farmer, he sent a pair of Spanish merino sheep, especially prized for the quality of their wool. To James Madison he sent books by the dozens, including a thirty-seven volume set of the *Encyclopedie Methodique*, which Madison called "a complete scientific library." Jefferson also sent him the works of Voltaire and other *philosophes*, which Madison devoured in preparing himself for the approaching constitutional convention. Madison reciprocated by sending Jefferson lengthy letters describing the movement to reform and strengthen the American government.

In 1786 Madison conveyed a request from the Virginia assembly that Jefferson find an architect for a new state capitol to be erected in Richmond. Jefferson responded by appointing himself. He would send plans, he told Madison, "taken from the best morsel of ancient architecture now remaining," a building that was "superior in beauty to anything in America, and not inferior to anything in the world." He had in mind the Maison Carré, a perfectly proportioned temple built by the Romans at Nîmes, in southern France. When he had first encountered the structure on one of his travels, Jefferson wrote to a French friend: "Here I am, Madame, gazing whole hours at the Maison Quarree like a lover at his mistress." By using classical forms Jefferson hoped to set a style for public buildings in America, improving the taste of his countrymen by teaching them in brick and stone the principles of great art. He also saw it as a declaration of intellectual independence, a break from the ponderous baroque style then common in Britain. It would be, he thought "an object and proof of national good taste." Yet Jefferson was not content simply to imitate the Roman temple. Many of its features were too ornate for the pristine values of a republic. In the columns that held the front portico he used unadorned Ionic capitals in place of the Corinthian tops preferred by the Romans. The result was a structure elegant in its simplicity, an architectural statement of republican values. With Madison providing the leadership in the assembly, the design was accepted, and the Virginia capitol became, as Jefferson had hoped, a model for public architecture in America.

The fits of depression returned in mid-1786. "I am burning the candle of life without present pleasure or future object," he told an American friend. Then, suddenly, on a late summer day there appeared a cure for his gloom in the form of Maria Cosway, whose beauty, grace, and mass of golden hair had been the rage of fashionable London for several seasons. She appeared on the arm of John Trumbull, the young Connecticut artist who had come to Europe to study with the masters and depict, from his imagination, the heroic scenes of the Revolution. She had been born in Italy of English parents and had earned a modest reputa-

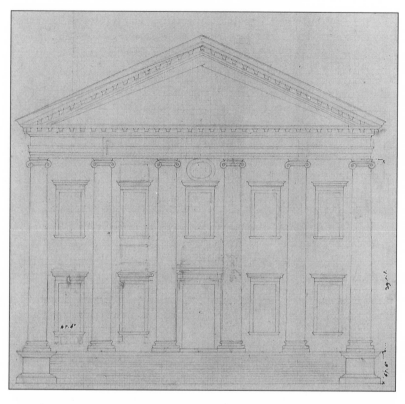

The Virginia Capitol, Richmond: Front elevation. By using
Ionic capitals on his columns (his model had Corinthian ones)
and adopting an unadorned frieze, Jefferson converted a
Roman temple into a meetinghouse for a pristine republic.
Courtesy of the Massachusetts Historical Society.

tion as a painter and musician. When her father's death left her
penniless, she entered into a marriage of convenience with Richard Cosway, the foremost miniature painter of the day, who
treated Maria with indifference. Finding that this was Mrs.
Cosway's first visit to Paris, Jefferson insisted on showing them
the sights with his own carriage. The ambassador's appointments
were canceled, and the party rode off to visit the royal park at St.

Cloud. When the day ended, Jefferson was so enchanted that he could not bear to part from the Cosways. His brain cooperated with his heart in devising plans, and after dinner they visited a pleasure garden designed by Italians whose specialty was "pantomimes" and fireworks. Still unwilling to part company and discovering Maria's interest in music, Jefferson took the party to the home of a teacher-composer for the harp, whose wife was thought to be the best harpist in Europe. When parting at last became inevitable, Jefferson extracted a promise that the Cosways would accompany him on similar expeditions.

There ensued a month-long romance, as day after day Jefferson's carriage stopped at the Cosways' house before embarking on a six- or seven-hour trip into the environs of Paris. Mr. Cosway and Trumbull soon dropped out and returned to their painting, but the lack of chaperones seemed not to trouble either Maria or Jefferson. The blissful moments ended abruptly in mid-September when the Cosways packed their things and set off for Antwerp, from whence they would take ship to England. After seeing them off, Jefferson, confessing that he felt "more dead than alive," returned to his lonely house and composed the most revealing, sentiment-filled letter of his letter-filled life. Utilizing one of the literary conventions of the day, Jefferson composed a dialogue between his head and his heart, initiated by the head who blamed the heart for its "warmth and precipitation," whose "follies" got them into "one of the scrapes into which you are ever leading us." The heart responded by reminding the head that its calculated plans had enabled them to hold on to the lady's presence on the day they first met. And so it went, page after page—too long, in fact, and eventually tedious to the modern reader. The ardor of Jefferson's message probably embarrassed and may have frightened the lady. She responded with a brief note, in Italian, expressing her dislike of London and desire to be "in the company of pleasant friends." When she returned to Paris in the spring, Mrs. Cosway found herself with too many engagements to see much of Jefferson. Before long even their correspondence ceased. The lady was in this instance the wiser of the two; in a time when divorce was well nigh impossible, a deeper involvement would have brought trouble, and probably grief, upon them both.

During that spring of 1787 Jefferson decided to bring another female into his life, ten-year-old Polly. This would complete his family circle and put some European polish on the stripling. It turned out to be more difficult than he had anticipated. Unlike most fathers of the eighteenth century, Jefferson would not simply order his daughter to come. He sought to persuade her, and this required all of his formidable rhetorical powers. The girl understandably did not want to undertake a long ocean voyage by herself or visit a foreign land with a strange language. Jefferson's promise of as many French dolls and playthings as she wanted was insufficient enticement. She wanted to stay in the comfortable home of Aunt Eppes. The baffled father eventually had to resort to trickery. He bought passage on a vessel departing from Baltimore. Aunt Eppes took Polly and her own children to the ship several days before its departure. The children were allowed to play about the ship; Polly fell asleep the night before departure and awoke to find herself at sea. She was accompanied by Sally Hemings, a slave girl of fourteen and sister of Jefferson's newly trained French chef. Sally had been pressed into service when an older nursemaid became ill and was unable to make the transatlantic voyage.

Because Sally Hemings would later become a subject of malicious gossip among Jefferson's political enemies and a salacious subject for populist historians, some discussion of her relationship with Jefferson is in order. Sally, as well as her brothers, half-brothers, sisters, and her mother Betty, went to Monticello after the death of John Wayles, as part of Martha Jefferson's inheritance. Betty was a mulatto born of the union of an English ship captain and a Wayles slave girl. It is possible, though unproven, that Sally and her brothers were the children of John Wayles. Jefferson seems to have accorded them a special status at Monticello, but whether that stemmed from their birth or their capabilities is not clear. Certainly the Hemings were among the brightest and most enterprising of his slaves. Why else would he have trained one to be a French chef and entrusted another, at the tender age of fourteen to guide his infant daughter across the Atlantic? In any case, the special status accorded Sally would give rise, during Jefferson's presidency, to accusations that he had fathered children by her.

Polly quickly forgave, or forgot, the ruse that had put her aboard the vessel, and before long she was the pet of captain and crew. When the voyage ended in England, there was more trouble getting her to leave the ship. The captain took her to London and deposited her in the arms of John and Abigail Adams. Polly again quickly made herself at home, and Abigail, who had recently seen her only daughter married, was soon gushing to Jefferson that "I never felt so attached to a child in my Life on so short an acquaintance." Jefferson sent a servant to London to pry a weeping Polly away from a tearful Mrs. Adams. He placed her in the convent school with her sister where, he reported proudly to Mrs. Eppes, she quickly "became a universal favorite with the young ladies and the mistresses."

During the four months prior to Polly's arrival Jefferson toured southern France and northern Italy. The journey gave him new insights into the magnificence of the French countryside and the misery of most of its inhabitants. Shortly after arriving in France he had written home that "the great mass of people were suffering under physical and moral oppression," and even the nobility did not possess the happiness "which is enjoyed by every class of people" in America. On this and other journeys Jefferson made every effort to meet the French people, sometimes knocking on their doors and buying lunch in their kitchens. From southern France he wrote to Lafayette urging him to make a similar trip. "To do it most effectively you must be absolutely incognito," he wrote. "You must ferret the people out of their hovels as I have done, look into their kettles, eat their bread, loll on their beds under the pretense of resting yourself, but in fact to find if they are soft." Jefferson was probably better acquainted with the French people than any member of the French government, and he foresaw trouble for the regime in the oppressiveness of the nobility and the exactions of the clergy.

Although a student of architecture, he was unimpressed with

the Gothic cathedrals of France and Italy, which he dismissed as a "waste of money." If the Italians had spent on engineering what they spent on churches, he wrote, they would have pushed the Apennines into the Adriatic and created a land bridge "from Leghorn to Constantinople."

WHEN JEFFERSON RETURNED FROM HIS TOUR in the summer of 1787, he found the French government in a crisis (ironically, at the very moment when a convention in Philadelphia was mending the American government by drafting a federal constitution). Earlier that year King Louis XVI and his ministers confessed that the government verged on bankruptcy. He summoned an Assembly of Notables—aristocrats from all parts of France—to advise him as to how to escape his financial mess. Jefferson was pleased that his friend Lafayette was among those named, and this no doubt had prompted his advice that Lafayette become acquainted with the people. Jefferson urged Lafayette to push for reform of France's authoritarian regime, developing a limited monarchy modeled on that of Britain. Jefferson thought that a gradual evolution into constitutional government might prevent a more violent revolution.

This advice stood in sharp contrast to his reaction to violent upheavals in America. During the winter of 1786–1787 debtor farmers in Massachusetts had taken up arms against the county courts in an effort to prevent them from foreclosing on their farms. The uprising was suppressed by the state, but it nevertheless sent a shiver of apprehension down the eastern seaboard. In distant Virginia, George Washington fretted about the threat of popular uprisings and mob rule. Jefferson, when he learned of the incident, was more sanguine. He wrote to a friend that he thought "a little rebellion now and then is a good thing" because it reminded the rulers of the rights and needs of the people. "The tree of liberty," he said, "must be refreshed from time to time with the blood of patriots & tyrants. It is its natural manure." Jefferson often indulged in such flights of rhetoric when he took quill in hand to address a close friend. One suspects his advice to

Lafayette, who was faced with a genuine revolution, more accurately reflected Jefferson's philosophy of governmental change.

He also heartily approved of Madison's efforts to strengthen the American government. Madison had sent him detailed notes of the series of meetings, first at Mount Vernon in 1785, then at Annapolis in 1786, that led to the Federal Convention at Philadelphia in the spring and summer of 1787. When the Convention completed its work Madison sent Jefferson a copy of the new Constitution. Because the Constitution carefully balanced the need for effective government with devices to prevent the abuse of power, Jefferson approved the document. He had two primary objections, however. The first was the omission of a bill of rights. Congress had been given extensive powers over taxation, trade, and war, but there was an inadequate list of things it could not do. Because the opponents of the Constitution were making the same point and simultaneously demanding a second convention, Madison was forced to resist the suggestion. However, he was quietly coming to the conclusion that Jefferson was right, that rights might be guaranteed by amendments once the Constitution was in place. Jefferson's other objection was to the lack of any limitation on the re-eligibility of the president. Jefferson worried that the powers of the president were such that he could assure himself re-election for life. Madison, convinced that Washington would be the first president, professed himself to be unworried about the prospect of a dictatorship. (Washington did in fact establish a tradition that a president serve only two terms, which lasted until Franklin Roosevelt's bid for a third term in 1940. The Washington tradition is presently enshrined in the Twenty-second Amendment.) Through the fall and winter of 1787–1788 Madison and other friends kept Jefferson informed of the ratification process. The Constitution had polarized the electorate; supporters of the Constitution had taken the name Federalists, leaving the opponents with the label of Antifederalists. This split over principle and policy—the first such division on a national level—would lead a few years later to the birth of national political parties.

Although the requisite nine states had given their approval

by the time the Virginia convention was in session in June 1788, its assent was crucial. The state was evenly divided, and a formidable alliance of Patrick Henry and George Mason stood in opposition. Jefferson no doubt glowed with pride when friends described how "the great little Madison" had responded to Patrick Henry's torrential rhetoric with subdued but relentless logic. In truth, most delegates came to the convention committed, and neither Madison nor Henry had any significant impact on the outcome. The Constitution squeaked through the 368-man Virginia convention by a margin of ten votes.

With his own government apparently on a secure foundation, Jefferson turned his attention back to France. For a year the Assembly of Notables did nothing but wrangle, and in May 1789 the desperate king summoned the Estates General, a body comparable to the British Parliament but which had not met in more than a century. The three Estates—nobility, clergy, and commoners—totaled about 1,200 persons. Jefferson thought it was too large to be effective, especially when it had no rules of procedure, no habits of order, and would consist "of Frenchmen among whom there are always more speakers than listeners."

Jefferson attended the opening of the Estates General on the fifth of May, but he soon grew discouraged when the assembly could not even agree on its rules for voting. On July 10, 1789 Lafayette introduced a bill of rights, which Jefferson had helped compose. It drew heavily on the Declaration of Independence and Jefferson's draft constitution for Virginia. By then, unfortunately, it was too late for gradual evolution; events were getting out of hand. The third estate, representing the common people, declared itself the National Assembly. When the king attempted to disband them, the delegates met in the indoor tennis court at the royal palace of Versailles and took an oath, swearing that they would continue to meet until they had drafted a constitution for France. The nobility tried to bring in troops from distant parts of France and instantly faced a mutiny by the army. On the fourteenth of July a Paris mob stormed the Bastille, freed its prisoners and gruesomely murdered the governor. Lafayette became commander of the Paris militia and led a march on Versailles. He brought the king back to Paris where he became, in Jefferson's words "a passive machine in the hands of the National Assembly."

Jefferson was nevertheless optimistic. He thought the king's humiliation a good opportunity to reform the government and resolve the crisis. He urged Lafayette and his party to form "a wise constitution along the British model with the king guaranteed his hereditary title, with powers so large as to enable him to do all the good of his station and so limited as to restrain him from its abuse." Two years earlier, in an essay explaining and promoting the new Federal Constitution, Madison had used very similar phrases in describing the new American presidency.

The National Assembly had no experience in drafting a constitution, and it asked for Jefferson's help. Jefferson politely declined, realizing that it was inconsistent with his diplomatic status. However, at Lafayette's urging, he did allow his house to be used for a clandestine meeting of eight leaders who wanted to map strategy. The next morning Jefferson reported the meeting to the French foreign minister, assuring him that he had maintained a strictly neutral role in the discussion. Far from chastising Jefferson, the minister replied that he knew all about the meeting and urged him to attend future conferences. He was sure that Jefferson's cool head would do much to moderate the "warmer spirits."

Central to any reform of the government was the principle that each generation had an inherent right to revise its constitution—"le droit des generations qui se succedent," or "right of successive generations" as the Declaration proposed by Jefferson and Lafayette phrased it. The idea was not new; the dead hand—"mortmain"—of the past was a common theme of the Enlightenment. The Assembly debated the concept at length, and on August 11 put it in effect by abolishing the feudal privileges of the nobility throughout France. In the end, however, the Lafayette–Jefferson language on the rights of generations was dropped from the Declaration when it was finally approved on August 26.

If Jefferson was disappointed, he did not say so. Nevertheless, he could not put le droit des generations out of his mind, perhaps because it had so many implications for his own life. If a generation had a right not to be burdened by the injustice of the past, it had a right to be free of the debts of the previous generation. National debt, much of it dating from the wars for empire and the wasted decadence of Louis XV, had sparked the Revolution in France. Similarly, the American Revolution, in Jefferson's view, had liberated American society from bondage to British merchants and subservience to parliamentary regulations. On a personal level, Jefferson himself was shackled by debts inherited from his father-in-law and made worse by the monetary chaos of the 1780s. This was the context in which Jefferson drafted, on September 6, 1789, and sent to his friend James Madison, one of the most interesting letters of his life.

After explaining that he was hurriedly putting into writing a subject that had "come into my head," he stated his proposition: "that the earth belongs in usufruct to the living." He explained the principle in terms of debts. One generation did not have the right to pass on a public debt to the next, nor did a man have the right to pass on his debts to his descendants or consume the usufruct ("fruits") of his estate for generations to come. If he did, "then the lands would belong to the dead and not to the living, which would be the reverse of our principle." Although his "principle" was hardly new, having been debated by the Assembly all summer, Jefferson characteristically added elements of his own. What was original about Jefferson's "principle" was the emphasis on generations, rather than, say, people. "The people" as a whole never dies; it has a corporate immortality, whereas a generation is defined by time. Indeed, Jefferson, with his bent for mathematics, undertook to calculate its exact duration. Using tables of mortality compiled by Count Buffon, Jefferson concluded that a person's average life expectancy was 38 years. Thus, fifty percent of each generation was gone after 19 years, and it no longer had a claim to govern. Thus, constitutions and laws ought to be automatically revised and public debts paid off every 19 years. The implications were breathtaking! They were also impractical, as Madison pointed out. Having experienced the difficulty of pushing a single constitution through the American body politic, Madison was horrified at the notion that the ordeal should be repeated every 19 years.

No doubt disappointed by Madison's cool response, Jefferson did not bring up the subject again. But he did not discard it altogether. Indeed, the concept that "the earth belongs to the living" was in many ways central to his political philosophy. It was at the root of the social reforms he had achieved during the Revolution, and it became his ideological rudder when he re-entered public life in the 1790s. Central to Jefferson's opposition to the financial policy of Alexander Hamilton in the 1790s was Jefferson's abhorrence at the Hamiltonian notion that a permanent public debt could be a "public blessing." Repayment of the national debt was a major goal, and achievement, of Jefferson's presidency. In his second inaugural address in 1805 he insisted that even in times of war it should be possible "to meet within the year all the expenses of the year, without encroaching on the rights of future generations, by burdening them with the debts of the past." In the last years of his life he would revive the principle of *droit des generations* in his crusade to revise the Virginia constitution of 1776.

THE NATIONAL ASSEMBLY'S FAILURE to do more than take symbolic steps in reforming the *Ancien Regime* eventually left Jefferson disillusioned. Toward the end of September 1789, he wrote to John Jay, U.S. Secretary for Foreign Affairs, that the Assembly was proceeding too slowly in the drafting of a constitution. "The original vice of their numbers causes this, as well as a tumultuous manner of doing business." As a result, he told Jay, "the patience of a people, who have less of that quality than any other nation in the world, is worn threadbare." He concluded ominously: "Civil war is much talked of and expected." This was his last eyewitness comment on the French Revolution. Within a few weeks he was on his way home.

After five years abroad, Jefferson felt it was time to return to Virginia and put his plantation in order. Another consideration was his daughters. He feared that if they stayed much longer in

France, they would be aliens in their own country when they returned, without friends or interest in Virginia. Adding urgency to his concern was a letter from Martha announcing that she wished to become a Roman Catholic. Jefferson hurried to the convent, and after a long, and apparently cordial, interview with the abbess, he took both girls home. Jefferson personally supervised their schooling for the remainder of their time in France.

Once he had his daughters settled and his affairs in order, Jefferson planned to return to France as ambassador. No other American, he realized, had his credentials for dealing with the fluid political situation in that country; no other American had a better chance of maintaining friendly relations between the two allies. Nor was his mind changed by a letter from Madison discreetly inquiring whether he would accept a place in the new administration. Madison had been elected to the House of Representatives in the first federal elections, and he had emerged as the spokesman for the Washington administration in the first session of Congress in the summer of 1789. Throughout that summer Madison and Washington spent long hours together as they cooperated in fleshing out the Constitution with executive offices and a federal judiciary. Jefferson rejected Madison's suggestion and emphatically declared that he wished to remain as ambassador to France.

Jefferson and his daughters sailed for home on October 22, 1789, and made the up-wind crossing in twenty-nine days. No sooner had he landed than he saw reports in the newspapers that Washington planned to make him Secretary of State. The rumors were confirmed when Mrs. Eppes, with whom he planned to leave Polly, handed him a letter from the President. Washington told him that "private regard" as well as "public propriety" induced him to nominate Jefferson for this important post which "involves many of the most interesting objects of the executive authority." Indeed it did, for in addition to handling foreign affairs the Secretary of State would be given responsibility for patents, weights and measures, coinage, the census, and (ultimately) supervision of the nation's capital. To carry out these multiple assignments the Secretary was given four clerks and a translator. Jefferson's letter of reply neither accepted nor rejected the President's offer. It was instead an expression of deep personal devotion to Washington and the cause of good government that he represented.

A few days after Jefferson arrived at Monticello Madison appeared at his doorstep armed with a dozen reasons why he should accept the offer of the State Department. Madison listened patiently while Jefferson poured out all his fears—his hesitation about the political appointments that would be in his power, his dislike for administration and the thousand nit-picking details that it involved, and above all his distaste for political controversy. He would be far more useful, he thought, if he returned to France and aided that country in its search for liberty. Madison reminded him that liberty was not yet fully assured here at home. In the half-year since the new government was launched, he had found disturbing evidence that some of the people around the President wished to expand his powers further, perhaps even establish a monarchy. At the opening of Congress that spring the Senate had engaged in an unseemly discussion of how to address the President. Some of the titles proposed, Madison thought, hinted strongly of royalty. It was only at Madison's insistence that the Congress had settled on a simple, republican form of address: "The President of the United States." Jefferson had no riposte to this logic. After Madison reported this meeting to Washington, the President wrote another letter to Jefferson expressing his eagerness to have Jefferson in the cabinet. Jefferson capitulated and re-entered the political arena. He would find the game rougher than any he had ever experienced.

Chapter Four

———————————◯———————————

Birth of the
Republican Party

JEFFERSON WAS FORTY-SEVEN YEARS OLD on March 21, 1790 when he stepped off a ferry that had carried him across the Hudson River and made his way through the narrow streets of New York. Although it was a Sunday he presented himself immediately to the President at his home on "the Broadway" and announced himself prepared to take up his duties. The announcement proved premature, for within days he was flattened by one of his periodic fits of migraine. For more than a month he was confined to his bed in a darkened room in the small house he had rented in Maiden Lane.

Before this misfortune occurred Jefferson met the other members of the cabinet at a dinner Washington gave on his behalf. Among those present was thirty-five year old Alexander Hamilton, Secretary of the Treasury. The appointment of the youthful Hamilton had been a surprise to some, though in Washington's view, it was a natural choice. Born in the West Indies, Hamilton had been educated at King's College (Columbia), New York, and had married into a prominent New York family. He had served as an aide to Washington during the war and had obtained banking experience under the tutelage of the Philadelphia merchant Robert Morris, the Superintendent of Finance during the Revolution. Hamilton was such a quick student that in 1781, when Morris was contemplating a national bank, Hamilton drafted his own plan for a bank and submitted it

73

for Morris's perusal. Three years later Hamilton led a group of merchants in creating the Bank of New York. By 1789 no one in the country could have brought better credentials to the Treasury. The other secretary present—Congress had created only three executive departments in the summer of 1789—was Henry Knox, Washington's former general of artillery, whose Department of War was brought over intact from the Confederation government. Rounding out the party was Attorney General Edmund Randolph. Congress had established this post when it created a federal court system in 1789. Randolph had no department to administer; he served, rather, as the legal adviser of the President. His importance derived from his close personal relationship with Washington. He was of old Virginia family and had been an ally of Madison's in the movement for constitutional reform. As governor of Virginia, Randolph had led the state delegation at the Philadelphia Convention and had introduced the "plan" that had formed the basis for the Constitution. Dissatisfied with the extensive powers given the government by the Convention, he had declined to sign the Constitution. However, he changed his mind again during the ratification process. His waffling continued during the political controversies that attended Washington's presidency. Jefferson would eventually refer to him disgustedly as a "chameleon" who never showed his true colors.

When Jefferson arose from his sick bed he found the capital buzzing with political controversy occasioned by a rift between the administration and its floor leader in Congress, James Madison. To the surprise and dismay of Federalists (the supporters of the administration had retained the name adopted during the movement for a new Constitution), Madison had led an opposition in the House of Representatives to Hamilton's plans for addressing the Revolutionary War debt. In January, Hamilton had sent to Congress a Report on the Public Credit in which he proposed to exchange the securities and other certificates issued by the old Congress during the war for bonds issued by the government. Unlike the earlier issues of public paper, the new securities would hold their value because they would bear a fixed rate of interest payable at regular intervals and funded through tax revenue. Although the securities issued during the war had depreciated badly in the 1780s and most had ended up in the hands of speculators, Hamilton proposed to redeem them at face value. He argued that only by dealing fairly with past creditors could the government restore faith among moneyed men and borrow from them in the future. The fact that this meant a windfall to speculators bothered Hamilton not at all. For the most part, they were the wealthier people, and to Hamilton wealth meant power. By tying wealthy merchants and landowners to the new order, Hamilton hoped to strengthen the government and ensure the durability of the Constitution.

Most speculators were northern merchants, and that was what aroused the ire of Madison's constituency, which was southern and rural. He suggested that the government discriminate among its creditors, paying the present holders the current market value (which was about 50% of face value) and giving the remainder to the original holders who had been forced to sell out. The scheme seemed fair, but it was also impractical since the securities had changed hands many times. Congress overrode Madison's suggestion, and Hamilton's funding system became law.

Madison had better luck with the other facet of Hamilton's fiscal plan, a proposal that the federal government assume the war debts of the states. Hamilton argued that the debts had been incurred in the common fight, and it was only fair that they be paid off by the nation as a whole especially since the states lost the power to levy their own tariffs under the new Constitution. The politics of the matter was that state creditors would thereafter look to the federal government for relief. The federal government would gain added strength at the expense of the states.

Madison was again on his feet in opposition, and this time he received substantial support from other southern congressmen. Virginia and the Carolinas had been the main theater of fighting in the last years of the war. Their governments had been constantly on the move, and their records were in disarray. Southern congressmen feared, therefore, that their state treasurers would not be able to document all their wartime expenses, and their states would come up short in the exchange. Hamilton's proposal for the assumption of state debts was defeated in the House on four successive votes in the spring of 1790, by margins of two to five votes.

At that juncture, in May 1790, Jefferson arose at last from his sick bed and prepared to take up his duties. He was preparing to pay a call on the President when Hamilton accosted him. The Treasury Secretary looked like a man in utter despair. His normally commanding gaze was dull; his clothes, normally in the highest of New York fashion, were rumpled and dirty. For a half hour he walked Jefferson up and down in front of the house explaining how the opposition in Congress was endangering the whole federal experiment. Jefferson later described his reaction. He protested to Hamilton that he was "a stranger to the whole subject." Nevertheless, his diplomatic service, which had involved borrowing money from European bankers, had left him deeply concerned about the nation's credit. Accordingly, he lent Hamilton a sympathetic ear and suggested that the quarreling parties join him at dinner the following day.

After he spoke with Madison, Jefferson recognized that a bargain, advantageous to both sides, might be struck. Since its very first session in Philadelphia in 1774 the issue that had divided the Congress more than any other was the location of the federal capital. New York had held the honor since 1784, but that site was never satisfactory to southerners, who objected to its distant location and shivered through its winters. The debates over Hamilton's program, which were attended by noisy speculators, only reinforced Madison's distaste for New York's money-grubbing atmosphere. Both Maryland and Virginia had offered to cede land to Congress for the creation of a national capital, but a southerly move was complicated by the desire of Pennsylvanians for a return to Philadelphia.

Over Jefferson's dinner table a bargain was struck. The capital would be moved to Philadelphia where it would remain for ten years while a new capital was built on the banks of the Potomac River, the exact location to be determined by the President. In return, two Virginia congressmen switched their votes, and Congress approved the plan for the assumption of state debts. The two Virginians were Federalists whose districts bordered on the Potomac River, and they were no doubt happy to return to the party fold. Equally important, so far as the southerners were concerned, was that Hamilton's Treasury Department adopted a policy of accepting whatever evidence of debt the states could supply. Southerners not only got the capital—the President had selected a site on the Potomac, not far from Mount Vernon—they profited handsomely by the federal government's takeover of their debts. Months later, after he and Hamilton had become bitter political rivals, Jefferson complained to friends that he was "most ignorantly and innocently made to hold the candle" in the deal. He need not have protested; he and Madison had cut a deal of which a rug merchant could be proud.

The temporary relocation to Philadelphia was the price of Pennsylvania's support for the "Compromise of 1790." Washington was not happy with that feature of the bargain, because he feared the capital might remain there through sheer inertia or the subtle machinations of the Pennsylvanians. In his anxiety Washington asked Jefferson to supervise the rapid development of the site on the Potomac. The federal tract, soon to be named the District of Columbia, was a square, ten miles on a side, that straddled the Potomac River, though most of it was in Maryland. Although ceded by the two states, the land had to be purchased from its current owners. This proved to be deceptively easy because most of the land was owned by Daniel Carroll, a close friend of Washington's. Besides, Carroll and other landowners were happy to exchange their title to rural tracts for future city lots. Organizing and selling the lands in the District proved to be more time-consuming and frustrating.

Jefferson was in his element, however, when it came to designing the federal city. To plan the city Jefferson obtained the services of a French engineer, Pierre Charles L'Enfant. He sent L'Enfant the layout of several French, German, and Italian cities, sketches of which he had made during his travels, but he also encouraged L'Enfant to adopt a classical style with its emphasis on space, order, and visual impact. L'Enfant chose to model the American capital after Versailles, Parisian home of the French kings, with its grid pattern of streets, broken by diagonal boulevards that radiated out from the royal palace in the center. Jefferson himself presided over the competition for the design of the capitol building. He chose a plan submitted by Dr. William Thornton, whose chief experience had been the building of palatial homes for West Indian sugar planters. His concept of the nation's capitol was a rectangular structure of classical proportions, topped by a Roman dome. Jefferson liked it for its "grandeur, simplicity, and beauty." In the competition for the executive mansion Jefferson submitted a design of his own, under a pseudonym. It was modeled on a Palladian villa, with a dome and porticos, much like Monticello. Washington preferred a simpler, yet also essentially classical, design by Irish architect James Hoban. As a result of Jefferson's influence the new capital rising on the banks of the Potomac would contain more classical buildings than any city in the world outside of Rome itself.

To this point Jefferson had expected to work cooperatively with Hamilton and other members of the President's cabinet, notwithstanding the warning of some Virginians that monarchists were plotting to subvert the government. An international crisis in the summer of 1790 awakened him to the profound differences in political philosophy that divided him from Hamilton. The controversy involved an inlet in the Pacific Northwest (Vancouver Island) called Nootka Sound. The waterway lay in a sort of no-man's-land between Spanish California and Russian Alaska. Great Britain had sought to establish a claim of its own in between these two toothless giants by settling a colony of men on Vancouver Island. The colony would also enable the British Hudson Bay Company to extend its fur trading operations into the Pacific Northwest. When a Spanish fleet captured the expedition, war seemed imminent, and both sides appealed for help from the United States. Specifically, the British wanted permission, in the event of war, to send an expedition from Canada down the Mississippi River to seize Spanish New Orleans. The crisis was Jefferson's first test as Secretary of State.

Jefferson's position was that any concession from the United States ought to come at a price, and there was much he wanted from both Britain and Spain. His idea was to send emissaries to both powers with orders to bargain for concessions. From Spain he wanted the free navigation of the Mississippi and the right to ship the produce of Tennessee and Kentucky through the port of New Orleans. Spain, which had regained control of Florida and the Gulf Coast in the Treaty of Peace ending the Revolution, prohibited Americans from using the lower Mississippi and the port of New Orleans. From Britain Jefferson wanted the cession of the outposts on the Great Lakes, such as Oswego on Lake Ontario, Niagara, and Detroit. Although these forts were on American territory and had been given to America in the treaty, Britain had refused to surrender them at the end of the Revolution, and in fact used them to arm and incite Native American tribes. The British claimed that they held the forts in retaliation for the refusal of Americans, mostly Virginians, to pay the prewar debts owed to British merchants. Jefferson, who was among the debtors, professed himself ready to pay the debt, but he refused to pay the interest that had accumulated during the war when it had been impossible to make payments. He also saw no connection between debts and forts. Jefferson's policy, in essence, was to take advantage of the quarrels of Europe in order to promote America's national interests.

To Jefferson's mounting exasperation Hamilton opposed this policy. He too wanted to promote the national interest, but he saw that interest in quite another way. He pointed out that America's principal trading partner was the former mother country, and that for the foreseeable future the United States would be dependent on British goods and British credit. Only by maintaining good relations with Britain, he argued, could the United States obtain the investment capital that it needed to grow and expand. Thus he would side with Britain in the controversy, even to the point of signing a formal alliance. Jefferson was appalled because, in his view, Hamilton's policy would turn back the Revolution. One purpose of independence, in the view of Jefferson and other Virginians, had been to end the cycle of dependence on British merchants and their agents. Hamilton's policy would place the nation once again in a posture of colonial dependency. The Nootka Sound crisis ended as swiftly as it had arisen, and the differences between Hamilton and Jefferson were momentarily shelved. However, the battlelines within the administration had been drawn.

The contest was soon resumed, this time on domestic policy. When Congress reassembled in December 1790, Hamilton was ready with two more reports. A Second Report on the Public Credit proposed the levy of excises, chiefly on distilled spirits, to sustain the debt that Hamilton had amassed. These passed with relatively little controversy, although the whiskey tax would ultimately cause rebellion west of the mountains. The other was a Report on a National Bank, which Hamilton envisioned as the capstone of his fiscal system. Modeled on the Bank of England, the bank (subsequently named the Bank of the United States) would be a partnership of business and government, in which the government would own one-fifth of the stock, and the President would name one-fifth of the board of directors. The bank would serve as the fiscal agent of the Treasury in collecting and dispersing funds, and its notes (backed by gold and Treasury bonds) would be legal tender in payment of all obligations to the government.

In Congress, Madison again took the lead in opposition. His chief objection was that the bank cemented the bond between the government and northern merchants. Madison had long been an advocate of strong, effective government, but he did not like the direction in which Hamilton was warping the government's powers. Rather than attack Hamilton's alliance with business interests directly, he objected to the bank on constitutional grounds when he took the floor of the House in February 1791. Madison pointed out that authority to charter private corporations was not among the delegated powers of Congress. Indeed, the Federal Convention had debated whether to give Congress that authority and had decided against it. Nevertheless the Hamiltonians were in the saddle, and Congress swiftly approved the bill chartering the Bank, for a twenty-year period.

Alexander Hamilton (1757–1804) was Jefferson's main opponent in Washington's cabinet and the focus of growing Republican dissatisfaction with the administration.

Madison's argument at least raised some doubts in the mind of Washington, and he decided to consult his cabinet before signing the bill. Jefferson, joined by Edmund Randolph, followed Madison's reasoning and argued for a narrow construction of the Constitution. He would limit the government's activities to those explicitly authorized by the Constitution. Hamilton, who had the advantage of seeing the opinions of Jefferson and Randolph before composing his own, took a novel tack. He pointed to a clause that gave Congress power to pass any laws that were "necessary and proper" to carrying out its other powers. This phrase meant, he maintained, that, in addition to its specifically delegated powers, Congress had certain "implied powers" to carry out its duties effectively. Implied in the delegated power to issue money, collect taxes, and pay its debts, for instance, was the power to create a bank for that purpose. Hamilton, in essence, was arguing that the Constitution was an elastic document, capable of being shaped to meet the changing needs of the country. Jefferson might have accepted this argument (as he eventually did when he became president) were he not concerned that the chief beneficiaries of this elasticity were Hamilton and his mercantile friends. For the moment, he felt that a strict adherence to the letter of the Constitution was the only defense to Hamilton's ambition. In the end, Hamilton's well-reasoned argument dispelled Washington's doubts, and he signed the bank charter into law. The controversy nevertheless brought into focus the philosophical gap between Jefferson and Hamilton. Hamilton was working on a mercantilist model of cooperation between business and government, in which the wealthy and powerful enjoyed special favor.

Jefferson regarded mercantilism as an "unnatural" policy that provided governmental awards to "parasites." Drawing on Country party ideology, as he had in the years before the Revolution, Jefferson predicted that Hamilton's largesse would lead to a spirit of acquisitiveness that in turn would lead to luxury and corruption. The prediction seemed to be borne out when the Bank began selling its stock on July 4, 1791. A subscriber could purchase a $400 share of stock by paying one-fourth in specie and the remainder in public securities. The Bank's entire offering was gone within an hour. The reason was an installment system which allowed an investor to pay only $25 for each share of stock to be delivered. He received scrip in return, which entitled him to so many shares, which he would pay for in installments. Because the scrip was transferable and could be purchased with previously worthless government securities, a furious speculation ensued. By the first of August government securities reached par, i.e., their face value equaled their market price. In a sense, this dramatized the success of Hamilton's system, but Jefferson and Madison saw in it nothing but evil. "It is impossible to say," Jefferson told Monroe, "where the appetite for gambling will stop." Even Virginians, or at least the mercantile element among them, were not immune. On July 24 he reported to Madison that "several merchants from Richmond (Scotch, English, &c.) were here lately. I suspect it was to dabble in federal filth."

Jefferson and Madison did not oppose commerce as such, but they did fear the commercialization of the country, with its ever-increasing gap between rich and poor. Such a development, they felt, would threaten the very existence of the republic, just as it had ruined the Roman republic. To Jefferson's alarm, Madison replied: "my imagination will not attempt to set bounds to the daring depravity of the times." By August Madison was certain that "The stock-jobbers will become the pretorian band of the Governmert, at once its tool & its tyrant; bribed by its largesses, & overawing it by clamours & combinations."

To meet this threat, Jefferson looked, in classic Country fashion, to yeomen farmers, small property holders devoted to the spirit of virtuous industry and resistant to the enticements of luxury. Because they owned their own land and depended for subsistence only on their own toil, they were free of fiscal temptations and marketplace corruption. Yet the Country rhetoric that came so easily to his lips masked a more subtle change in his thinking. Farmers and planters, after all, were dependent on the marketplace; commerce was essential to the national well-being. The threat, he was coming to realize, was not from commerce, but from privilege.

Commercial independence from Europe, which he had fought for all his political life, was one thing; commercial domination of the political and social fabric was quite another. Jefferson was beginning to see a future in which government and business were separate spheres, and business enterprise took place on a level playing field where no one enjoyed government favor or special privilege. This concept—quite radically different from Country ideology because it looked to the future, rather than the past—was never fully articulated in the 1790s. But it became his guiding beacon after he became president, at a time when, significantly enough, he regarded corruption as no longer a serious threat to the republic.

THE PHILOSOPHICAL DISPUTE TURNED to personal animosity as Jefferson gradually realized that Hamilton was interfering in the affairs of the State Department. During the Nootka Sound crisis Hamilton revealed that he was in contact with Major George Beckwith, a British agent who had been sent to New York by the governor of Canada. Britain had contemptuously left vacant the post of ambassador to the United States since the end of the war. Beckwith was the only envoy available, and Hamilton had quickly struck up a friendship with him. Hamilton even represented to the cabinet—falsely—that the idea of a formal alliance had come from Beckwith. In the wake of the war scare Britain dispatched an ambassador, George Hammond, with whom Hamilton quickly became as confidential as he had been with Beckwith. Jefferson suspected that Hamilton was keeping the British informed of every cabinet discussion that had to do with British policy. Historians with access to British state papers have confirmed the suspicion. When Jefferson prepared a lengthy paper demolishing the British excuses for failing to honor the peace treaty, Hamilton told Hammond—falsely—that Washington had not read the paper, and it did not represent the policy of the administration. The British never bothered to reply. Jefferson suspected that Hamilton was behind the British ambassador's serene intransigence, and his anger deepened.

By early 1791 the circle of congressmen that looked to Madison for leadership had begun referring to themselves as "republicans." The choice of name revealed their deepest concern—that the Washington administration, in its drive to enhance federal power, was tipping the country toward a monarchy. The "republicans" were not yet a political party, for they lacked any support outside the halls of Congress. Indeed, most people, even in the capital city, were unaware of the rift between Jefferson and Hamilton and the close cooperation of Jefferson with Madison. A series of incidents in the spring and summer of 1791 brought the schism in the government to public attention and impelled both sides to seek popular support.

Hamilton was first to see the value of newspaper support. When the government moved to Philadelphia, he earnestly courted the favor of John Fenno, editor of the city's largest newspaper, *The Gazette of the United States*. Fenno probably would have been a Loyalist had he been prominent during the Revolution, for he had an open contempt for popular rule and republican forms of government. "Take away thrones and crowns from among men, and there will soon be an end of dominion and justice," he intoned. Hamilton not only provided Fenno with inside news and essays of his own composition; he urged his friends to subscribe to the paper and even paid some of Fenno's bills. He received in return effusive praise and editorial endorsement of his every program.

Jefferson, who complained of Fenno's "pure toryism," was dismayed to see his old revolutionary comrade, John Adams, now vice president, appear in Fenno's sheet. Adams had written a series of essays called "Discourses on Davila," an elaboration of political theory, based on the writings of an Italian historian. Adams revealed a clear admiration for the form of the British government, and he predicted that France was doomed unless its revolutionaries could work out a system of balanced government similar to that of England organized around the king, lords, and commons. To Jefferson, Adams appeared to be endorsing Hamilton's idea of a Senate that was elected for life and controlled by the nouveau elite being created by Hamilton's fiscal favoritism.

Jefferson still was smoldering over the apostasy of his old friend, when he received from Europe a copy of Tom Paine's *Rights of Man*. Paine, the propagandist of the American Revolution, had moved to France and was lending his quill to the service of the French Revolution. More than a defense of the events in France, Paine's pamphlet was a clarion call for revolution based on reason, one that would eliminate such irrational appendages as inherited privilege and established religion. Jefferson heartily approved, and when he sent the book to a Philadelphia printer who had expressed an interest in publishing it, he added a friendly note saying that he was "extremely pleased to find it will be re-printed here, and that something is at length to be publicly said against the political heresies which have sprung up among us." He added that he had "no doubt our citizens will rally a second time round the standard of Common sense." The printer could not pass up an endorsement by the Secretary of State, and, without asking Jefferson's permission, he printed the note on the frontispiece. Jefferson was surprised and embarrassed, realizing that John Adams was the person most likely to be offended. He quickly wrote letters to the President and to Adams, explaining how the mistake had come about. Adams replied warmly to the gesture of friendship and accepted Jefferson's explanation. However, the relations between the two would not again be the same. More important, the incident brought to public attention the rift within the government, and, although Madison had initiated the opposition, Jefferson was thereafter identified as its leader.

The terms "party" and "faction" were used synonymously in the eighteenth-century political discourse, and both were pejorative terms. They denoted groups of men with sinister objectives, who worked the legislative halls for their own selfish ends, rather than for the common good. Madison's correspondence in mid-1791 reveals a subtle change in his concept of "party," a dawning realization that opposition to ministerial policies was not necessarily detrimental to the republic. He began to realize that it was possible to oppose certain policies of the men in power, while remaining loyal to the government—that is, the Constitution—itself. This concept would be the foundation for a party system, a wholesome competition among parties for control of the government.

Hand in hand with the concept of a political party came the realization that Republicans needed to broaden the basis of their support. To this point the Madison circle in the House of Representatives consisted of a handful of southerners, most of them from Virginia and North Carolina. Consequently, in early 1791 Jefferson began tentative efforts to identify potential adherents. One of his first targets was George Mason, famed as the author of Virginia's Declaration of Rights and an opponent of the Constitution. Hinting that Mason might wish to return to politics, Jefferson suggested that "the only corrective of what is corrupt in our present form of government will be the augmentation of the numbers in the lower house, so as to get a more agricultural representation, which may put that interest above that of the stock-jobbers." He was more open with James Innes, attorney general of Virginia, urging him to run for Congress, having "such confidence in the purity of your republicanism, that I know your efforts would go in a right direction."

In May 1791 Jefferson and Madison departed for the north, hoping to make some political contacts. They targeted New York, in particular, for that state had been evenly divided on the Constitution, and its perennial governor, George Clinton, was an opponent of Hamilton and his Federalist friends. Federalist Robert R. Livingston, New York's chancellor, was also alienated from the Hamiltonians. The "cover story" was that it was a scientific expedition. The Hessian fly, arrived from Europe in the mid-1780s, was doing considerable damage to northern cereal crops, and the American Philosophical Society, of which Jefferson had recently been elected vice president, wished to study the pest. Jefferson was also interested in the "botanical objects" of a part of the country he had never visited.

One early contact was Philip Freneau, a New Jersey farmer and poet, who had been a classmate of Madison's at Princeton. They persuaded Freneau to move to Philadelphia to found an anti-administration newspaper, *The National Gazette,* which, they hoped, would counter the "poison" that emanated from Fenno's *Gazette.* Jefferson offered him the translator's position in the State Department at an annual salary of $250, which was expected to keep Freneau alive until his newspaper was established. Freneau agreed with the stipulation that he have complete control over the contents of his newspaper.

The trip took a little more than a month and covered 920 miles. The Virginians sailed up the Hudson River, crossed Lake George and Lake Champlain, and returned to New York City by way of Vermont, Connecticut, and Long Island. As he habitually did on his travels, Jefferson made copious notes on the trees and plants foreign to Virginia, and wrote long letters to his daughters on the beauty of Lake George and the Adirondack mountains. But there was political business as well. Although Governor

Clinton took no notice of the Virginians, and they made no effort to contact him, they did pay a visit to Robert R. Livingston, owner of vast estates in the Hudson River Valley and former Secretary for Foreign Affairs in the Confederation. Jefferson, in fact, had opened a correspondence with Livingston that spring and found him a potential ally. Livingston had discovered that the landed gentry he represented in New York had become poor relations to the moneyed elite who profited so much by Hamilton's fiscal policies. In addition, Hamilton had cut the Livingston clan off from federal offices. As a result, in January of that year Livingston had joined forces with the Clintonians in the legislature to elect Aaron Burr to the United States Senate in place of Hamilton's father-in-law, Philip Schuyler. In New York City, the Virginians paid a visit to Burr, and Federalists were soon reporting to Hamilton that there was a "passionate courtship" among Livingston, Burr, and the two Virginians. There is no evidence of any bargains struck or alliances made, but the tour laid the foundation for a "New York–Virginia axis" that would be the centerpiece of the Jeffersonian Republican Party throughout its history. Until 1824 a succession of Virginia presidents would choose New Yorkers for their vice presidents. An early hint of this interstate alliance came in the presidential election of 1792. Washington was re-elected without opposition, but Virginia and North Carolina gave their vice presidential electoral ballots to George Clinton.

FRENEAU'S ATTACKS ON THE ADMINISTRATION, including, for the first time, criticism of the President himself, triggered a war of words. Writing under various pseudonyms, Hamilton replied in the columns of Fenno's *Gazette*. Not content with defending himself, Hamilton named Jefferson as the instigator of political discord. Although Jefferson himself declined to do battle, his Virginia friends responded to Hamilton in kind. The journalistic warfare kept the public apprised of the rift in the government, but it did little to bring adherents to either side. Few, outside of Philadelphia, understood the implications of Hamilton's alliance with northern merchants; fewer still understood the intricacies of his fiscal policy. In the end, it was not Hamiltonian finance but the outbreak of war in Europe that brought about the formation of political parties in America. The European war, which pitted republican France against a coalition of monarchies led by Britain, was pregnant with symbolism—monarchy versus republic, civil order versus mob violence—symbols that were easily put to partisan use in America.

Americans generally applauded the early stages of the French Revolution because the French seemed to be moving in the direction of a constitutional monarchy with guarantees for the rights of its citizens. However, the rulers of France's neighbors, Prussia and Austria, thought otherwise, and they threatened intervention to preserve the powers and status of Louis XVI. The French king secretly encouraged their intrigues. In April 1792 the Legislative Assembly preempted Austria and Prussia by declaring war first. Americans again generally approved, and when French armies scored some early victories, there were public celebrations from Boston to Charleston. In September 1792 the Assembly lost patience with Louis, abolished the monarchy, and transformed itself into a convention that announced the establishment of the French Republic.

Some Americans began to have doubts when, in early 1793, the National Convention found Louis XVI guilty of treason and executed him and later his queen Marie Antoinette. The entry of Britain into the war shortly thereafter, further divided Americans and caused an earnest debate within the President's cabinet. All agreed that the United States ought to stay out of the war. The issue was whether American neutrality ought to be formally proclaimed, and if so, whether it ought to carry a price tag. The problem was complicated by the treaty of alliance with France signed by Benjamin Franklin during the Revolution. The treaty did not oblige the United States to send an army to Europe, but it did oblige the U.S. to aid in the defense of French islands in the West Indies if they were attacked. A quick decision was required, for the French republic had sent an emissary, Edmond

Genet, who was due to arrive in April. The question was how to receive him and how to answer his demands.

As usual, Jefferson and Hamilton were at loggerheads. Hamilton initially argued that the treaty had been negotiated with the French monarch, and it terminated with his death, but Jefferson convinced Washington that, under international law, treaties survived a change in government and that the United States was duty-bound to honor its obligations. Jefferson therefore argued that Britain could expect America to side with France and would gain immensely by American neutrality. Britain therefore ought to be made to pay a price for it; Jefferson thought the surrender of the Northwest posts a reasonable sum. Hamilton adhered to his position that the flow of commerce and capital from Britain was America's economic lifeline, and he thought the government should do nothing to jeopardize it. Even before the cabinet reached a decision, Hamilton privately assured the British minister that America would remain neutral. In the cabinet, Randolph and Knox sided with Hamilton in rejecting the idea of demanding concessions. After much wrangling the cabinet agreed on a presidential proclamation, one that avoided the word "neutrality" and simply ordered Americans to conduct themselves impartially in the international areana. The President issued it on April 22, 1793.

Genet, meanwhile, had landed in Charleston, South Carolina, a port of embarkation that foreign visitors did not normally use. Genet claimed that winds had driven his ship there, but one might be pardoned for assuming it was a "political wind." The point of arrival enabled Genet to make a triumphant tour northward through the Carolinas and Virginia where pro-French feeling ran high. When he announced on arrival that he did not seek America's entry into the war, he was handsomely entertained by the Charleston gentry, Republicans and Federalists alike. Taking his cue from the warm reception, he issued letters of marque to four French vessels, manned largely by American sailors, which enabled them, as privateers, to prey on British commerce under the French flag. He then began his progress northward, wined and dined at every carriage stop. Even news of the President's proclamation, which reached Genet in Richmond, did not chill the heady acclaim he was receiving. Philadelphia gave him a delirious reception that lasted for several days, after which he finally presented his credentials to the President. When Genet visited the State Department, Jefferson, adhering to the President's policy, told the Frenchman that the United States would not permit the dispatch of any more privateers.

The revolution in France took another radical turn in the summer of 1793. The entry of Britain and Spain into the war had turned the tide of battle. With foreign armies camped on French soil, a working class, extremist element, the Jacobins (after "Jacques," the generic nickname for French peasants) seized power. They arrested members of the French aristocracy and began to execute them using the dreaded guillotine. The "reign of terror" in France further polarized Americans. Federalists, ever fearful of mob rule, looked to Britain as the world's bastion for the defense of law and order. Jefferson was shocked at the bloodshed but inclined to look at the big picture. France, he had come to feel, might be the first line of defense for republican ideals in a world dominated by monarchies. When Jefferson's Parisian friend and neighbor, the Duke de la Rochefoucauld, was beaten to death by a Parisian mob, William Short, one-time secretary to Jefferson and currently minister to Holland, wrote Jefferson a critical report on the ominous tendencies of the revolution. Jefferson reproved him with the most emotional political statement he ever made. "The liberty of the whole earth was depending on the issue of the contest," he explained. He admitted that his "own affections have been deeply wounded by some of the martyrs to this cause." But rather than see it fail, "I would have seen half the earth desolated. Were there but an Adam and an Eve left in every country, and left free, it would be better than as it now is." Radical, even bloodthirsty, though this letter seems, it must be remembered that he expressed these sentiments to a close friend, who had experienced with him the heady idealism of the opening days of the Revolution. Jefferson was always careful to keep personal feelings separate from public policy. His personal emotions were ever subordinate to his guiding political principle—American national interest. Citizen Genet would learn this lesson the hard way.

His head turned by the reception he had received on the way to Philadelphia, Genet impertinently rejected Jefferson's communication that the government would not allow the further arming of privateers. He told the astonished Secretary that he would accept the President's "political opinions" only until such time as Congress met and rejected them. Jefferson's effort to instruct the Frenchman on the way the U.S. government worked fell on deaf ears. With unbelievable effrontery Genet warned Jefferson that he spoke for the American people, whose "fraternal voice has resounded from every quarter around me!" Jefferson passed these outrageous communications on to the cabinet, only to suffer further humiliation when Hamilton used them as ammunition to pursue his own pro-British agenda.

In early July Jefferson received fresh evidence of Genet's arrogance. Pennsylvania authorities informed him that the *Little Sarah*, a British brigantine brought into Philadelphia by a French warship, was being transformed into a privateer. Fourteen cannon had been put aboard, and Genet had renamed it *La Petite Democrate*. On the evening of July 6, Alexander J. Dallas, the Pennsylvania Secretary of State, paid a visit to Genet's house to request that he not allow the *Little Democrat* to put to sea. Genet flew into a rage, refused to detain the ship, and threatened to appeal to the people over the President's head. Next Jefferson called on Genet himself. When he suggested that Genet detain the vessel, he was greeted by a torrent of revolutionary rhetoric. Convinced that Congress was on the side of France, Genet threatened to demand that Washington call it back into session. Jefferson went home and poured out his frustration to Madison. "Never in my opinion," he wrote, "was so calamitous an appointment made as that of the present Minister of France here. Hotheaded, all imagination, no judgment, passionate, disrespectful and even indecent toward the P. in his written as well as verbal communications. . . . He renders my position immensely difficult."

A few days later Genet sent the *La Petite Democrate* to sea

armed with a French letter of marque. When Jefferson informed
the cabinet, Hamilton wanted to take a hard line with the French
by publishing the correspondence and peremptorily demanding
Genet's recall. Jefferson wished to avoid alienating the French
government. He proposed that they send Genet's outrageous
letters to Paris accompanied by "friendly observations," on the
assumption that France would promptly recall its wayward minister. More vexing to Washington than Genet's behavior was the
journalistic criticism of him that Genet's arrival had triggered.
Led by Freneau, the Republican press had become ever more
personal in its abuse of the President, and Washington's skin was
far too thin to ignore it. In a cabinet meeting in early August he
interrupted the debate between Jefferson and Hamilton to ex-
plode in rage at the behavior of the American press, ending with
a tirade against "that rascal Freneau," who sent him three copies
of his paper every day, as if he expected the President to become
his "distributor."

The President's outburst ended the cabinet discussion, and
Jefferson was left to devise his own policy. He sent copies of
Genet's correspondence to Paris accompanied by a delicate letter
that simply summarized the situation. By then the Jacobins had
seized power in France, and they were moving to execute the
Girondin officials who had originally dispatched Genet. They
were only too happy to recall Genet. Unwilling to face the
guillotine, Genet decided to become an immigrant, and, despite
his excesses, Washington let him stay. He settled in New York,
took up farming, and married the daughter of Governor George
Clinton.

Before settling into private life, however, he committed one
final outrage. He sent some of his correspondence with Jefferson
to the newspapers, evidently still in the hope that the American
people would rally to his cause. Realizing that Americans were
far more likely to rally around the President, Jefferson warned
Republicans that they must dissociate themselves from the "in-
corrigible" Frenchman. He told Madison that Republicans should
"approve unequivocally of a state of neutrality . . . [and] abandon
Genet entirely, with expressions of strong friendship & adher-

ence to his nation & confidence that he has acted against their sense." Jefferson concluded with one of his more memorable aphorisms: "In this way we shall keep the people on our side by keeping ourselves in the right." Madison conferred with James Monroe, and the pair organized a series of popular meetings in Virginia which produced sets of resolutions denouncing Genet while expressing sympathy for France. The damage control worked. Republicans suffered only a momentary setback in their drive for popular support.

The Genet affair closed Jefferson's career as Secretary of State. Even at the height of the crisis his thoughts were never far from the land. On July 7, 1793, after his stormy visit with Genet, he wrote Martha from his temporary home on the outskirts of Philadelphia, "I never before knew the full value of trees. My house is entirely embosomed in high plane trees, with good grass below, & under them I breakfast, dine, write, read, & receive my company. What would I not give that the trees planted nearest round the house at Monticello were full grown." On July 31 he informed Washington of his determination to retire. Washington expressed some bitterness that, after persuading him to undertake a second term, both Jefferson and Hamilton planned to leave the government (Hamilton resigned in January 1795 to resume his law practice). The President persuaded Jefferson to see it through to the end of the year. Jefferson agreed, concluded the Genet business, and resigned effective December 31, 1793. Once again he returned to Monticello and his daughters with plans never again to leave either.

FOR A TIME HE MADE GOOD ON HIS RESOLVE. He did not write a single letter on the subject of politics for three months. He spent the time rebuilding his farms and enjoying the company of his grandchildren, Anne Cary Randolph, now three years old, and Thomas Jefferson Randolph, two. In the spring of 1794 he wrote a friend that his days were spent "in my farmer's coat, immersed soul and body in the culture of my fields, and alive to nothing abroad except successes of the French Revolution, and the wel-

Ink wash sketch of Monticello, by Robert Mills, ca. 1803. As a result of Jefferson's additions in the 1790s, the building on "Little Mountain," was complete at last. *Courtesy of the Massachusetts Historical Society.*

fare of my friends." Despite this idyllic existence, his fertile mind remained active. Throughout his political career he had sought ways of making Virginia—and the United States—economically independent. In furtherance of this aim, and with an eye on his own balance sheet, he started up a nail factory at Monticello. He personally supervised the training of a dozen young male slaves. Through a combination of persuasion, praise, and cash bonuses, his nailery was soon producing a ton and half of nails a month.

The nail factory proved more than a source of income. It gave Jefferson an opportunity to observe the abilities and attitudes of his young slaves and gauge their potential for training. The plantation required a variety of artisan skills: carpenters, blacksmiths, shoemakers, woodcutters, and charcoal burners. Young men with ambition to do something besides field work had a chance, through their performance in the naillery, to influence their futures. Most eventually occupied the most important artisan and household positions on the "little mountain."

Jefferson sold his nails to storekeepers and planters throughout Virginia, but often he was his own best customer. Among his projects in retirement was the completion of Monticello, which, despite the grand design he had devised twenty years earlier, was still little more than a country farmhouse. Always a devotee of Palladian forms, he had seen in Paris how this style lent an aura of elegance to the low, unpretentious townhouses of the French aristocracy. He had seen how second floors constructed as mezzanines gave the house an appearance of being a single story while greatly adding to the grandeur of the first floor. He had also learned how the addition of a modest dome could grace a private residence without making it pretentious. He added all these elements to Monticello and in the process enlarged the house to almost three times its original size. He achieved the one-story effect by nestling the house into the side of the hill and by blending the windows of the main floor with those of the mezzanine floor. The second story, which had originally housed his library, was remade into bedrooms to accommodate the many friends, relatives, and foreign travelers that kept him company. The work was not done all at once, and, indeed, it continued even into his presidency. However, a drawing made by Jefferson in 1796, complete with specifications down to the last detail, embodied the mature concept.

The work on Monticello required artisan skills that were not readily available in Virginia. Jefferson asked friends in Philadelphia and in Europe to be on the lookout for the best stonemasons and woodworkers. These workmen in turn imparted their knowledge to the blacks who worked as their assistants. John Hemings, Sally's brother, learned woodworking from an Irish immigrant that Jefferson had hired. Together they crafted Monticello's interior woodwork, to which, Jefferson thought, "there is nothing superior in the US." Hemings reigned in the Monticello woodworking shop through the rest of Jefferson's life, and he was set free, along with several other artisans, by Jefferson's will.

Busy as he was, Jefferson gradually began to sense the effect on his personality of this rural isolation. Years later, he confided to his daughter Mary the effect that his retirement from public life had on him. "I remained closely at home," he recalled, "saw none but those who came there, and at length became very sensible of the ill effect it had upon my own mind. . . . I felt enough of the effect of withdrawing from the world then, to see that it led to an antisocial and misanthropic state of mind, which severely punishes him who gives in to it: and it will be a lesson I shall never forget as to myself."

The world of politics was in fact never far from his thoughts. Madison wrote him from the nation's capital as often as three times a week; Monroe and other Republicans kept him abreast of political happenings in Virginia. Six months after Jefferson retired from the State Department a western uprising further polarized the country and added new strength to Republican ranks. The excise of 1791, which levied heavy duties on distilled spirits, was immensely unpopular in the trans-Appallachian West, from Pennsylvania to Kentucky and Tennessee. Whiskey was more than a beverage to the frontiersmen; it was their only cash crop. Because of the primitive condition of the roads, it was not feasible to transport bulky crops of grain across the mountains to eastern markets. Only by converting it to whiskey could a pioneer farmer get his crop to market. As a result, nearly every pioneer farmer had a still and reckoned his wealth in "Monongahela Rye." The federal excise thus fell directly on them, and they had no means for paying it, even if they wished to, because there was no hard coin anywhere in the West. Throughout the West federal collectors were assaulted, and many resigned their posts.

Anxious to assert federal authority, Hamilton decided to make an example of western Pennsylvania, the one part of the frontier to which the government had road access. At his urging, Washington issued a proclamation denouncing the rebellion, and when that was ignored, the President sent an army of 15,000 into the Monongahela Valley under the command of Virginia Governor "Light Horse Harry" Lee. The "rebellion" evaporated, and its leaders could not be identified. Indeed, the most prominent men in the Valley, such as Albert Gallatin, had worked to prevent violence. The army arrested twenty obscure characters and paraded them, bound in ropes, back to Philadelphia. If there had ever been any doubt as to the political color of the West, there was no more. The West thereafter was Republican territory. To an indignant Jefferson, the heavy-handed actions of the government were further evidence of its drift into brutality and repression.

The smoke from the Whiskey Rebellion had barely cleared when a new political firestorm hit the nation. When Britain entered the European war in 1793, it declared a naval blockade of France. The Royal Navy enforced the blockade by seizing American vessels in the West Indies on the pretext that they were carrying French products destined for France. With Republicans in Congress calling for commercial retaliation and even war, Washington sent Chief Justice John Jay to Britain in a desperate effort to preserve the peace. Jay was to secure some sort of agreement on America's neutral rights on the high seas, as well as a resolution of problems lingering from the Peace Treaty, such as British retention of the Northwest posts.

In London, Jay was greeted by a ministry flushed with a sense of victory. The French had been at war with themselves in a year-long "reign of terror," and their navy had been destroyed. The ministry saw little reason to accommodate the United States. As a result, the treaty that Jay signed in November 1794 contained no reference to neutral rights. Jay did win a promise to evacuate the Northwest posts by 1796, and he obtained some trade concessions in the British West Indies. In return, he agreed to an international commission that would supervise the repayment of pre-Revolutionary debts owed to British merchants. Washington was not happy with the treaty, but he submitted it to the Senate anyway. Although the Senate hoped to keep it secret until it was formally ratified, Republicans leaked it to the press. The ensuing uproar was deafening. Each party mobilized its grass-roots support and organized popular meetings and petition campaigns. When the dust settled, the first party system was in place; scarcely a voter in the country failed to identify himself either as a Republican or a Federalist.

The public reaction to the treaty stemmed from the sectional incidence of its impact. The North gained the most by the British concessions; southern planters would pay the price. To Jefferson, however, the chief objection was the lack of guarantees for

American neutral rights. The legal vacuum left American ship-
pers at the mercy of the Royal Navy. In a larger sense, the failure
to define the right of free trade continued to leave the American
economy in a position of colonial dependence on the former
mother country. Despite the hope that political independence
would bring economic independence, despite Jefferson's effort
as ambassador to open a market for tobacco in France, Virginia
planters had refused to abandon the colonial system, and they
were as bound to British merchants as ever. Tobacco prices had
collapsed again in the early 1790s, and many planters faced ruin.
In Jefferson's view, the Jay Treaty prevented the United States
from ever winning its economic independence.

In the spring of 1796 Madison made a final effort to torpedo
the treaty by denying an appropriation of money needed to carry
out its terms. On the eve of the vote on the measure, Republicans in the House of Representatives held a party caucus—the
first ever—to ensure party unity. On the House floor the following day the motion to deny the appropriation failed by a single
vote. The even balance between the parties made it grimly clear
to Jefferson that if Republicans put forth a strong candidate they
would have a chance to win the presidency that year. On September 17 Washington informed the country that he would not
accept a third term; John Adams was the likely nominee of the
Federalist Party. Jefferson wistfully hoped that Madison might
agree to be the Republican candidate, but he conceded that
Madison was too scarred by the political warfare in the Congress.
Slowly Jefferson came to realize that only he had the national
stature to make a contest of it in a race against Adams. Jefferson
never announced his candidacy; he merely failed to make a
public withdrawal.

The campaign was conducted in the press by the partisan
adherents of each candidate. Neither Jefferson nor Adams made
a single speech, nor even a public comment. Washington had
established the tradition that a presidential candidate must not
appear to lust for office, and the tradition stood for more than a
century. The balloting, which went on for several weeks since
there was no single election day, was a seesaw affair, with Adams

carrying New England and Jefferson winning the South and West. They divided the middle states, and Jefferson carried Pennsylvania by a mere handful of votes. Anticipating that there might be a tie in the electoral vote, Jefferson wrote Madison to authorize him to yield the victory to Adams. "He has always been my senior," Jefferson explained, "from the commencement of our public life, and the expression of the public will being equal, this circumstance ought to give him the preference."

Unfortunately, neither Adams nor the American public ever learned of this unique gesture, for the electoral tie never materialized. Three states—Pennsylvania, Virginia, and North Carolina—chose their presidential electors by districts, and although Jefferson carried all three in the popular balloting, a single Federalist elector in each state cast a ballot for Adams. Adams thus won the election by 71 to 68. Jefferson, having come in second, was vice president under the electoral process set up by the Constitution. For the next four years he would be in the uncomfortable position of being the only Republican in a fiercely partisan Federalist administration.

Chapter Five

—————○—————

Reign of Witches

TROUBLED BY THE THOUGHT OF A LONG JOURNEY in February 1797, Jefferson at first hoped to skip Adams's inauguration. He felt that any senator could administer his oath of office as vice president whenever he arrived in Philadelphia. He quickly changed his mind, however, when he realized that his absence might be misinterpreted by his political foes and, worse, by the public. He nevertheless hoped to "escape into the city as covertly as possible" in order to avoid pomp and ceremony. Accordingly, he left his phaeton in Alexandria and took a public stage to Philadelphia. This hope too was frustrated. A troop of artillery met him at the city gate, signaled his approach with sixteen rounds from two twelve-pounders, and escorted him into Philadelphia under a banner inscribed "Jefferson, The Friend of the People." After spending the first night with the Madisons, Jefferson went to Francis's Hotel on Market Street, remaining there until he returned to Monticello ten days later.

Jefferson's first move on his arrival was to pay a call on John Adams. He was cordially received; both men felt their long-standing friendship had survived the political differences of the past few years. The next morning, March 3, Adams returned the call and immediately broached the problem of French relations. Adams had inherited from Washington a crisis with France, stemming from the Jay Treaty. Assuming that the treaty had made allies of the United States and Great Britain, France had refused to receive Charles Cotesworth Pinckney, whom Washington had sent to Paris as minister to replace James Monroe. French warships also began seizing American merchant vessels. Adams wanted to send a special envoy to assuage the French, and his thoughts had turned to James Madison, who had declined re-election to Congress and retired to his Virginia plantation, Montpelier. Impressed by Adams's spirit of accommodation, Jefferson agreed to sound out his friend. However, when he talked to Adams again, over dinner at Washington's house a few days later, he found that Adams had dropped the whole idea. Jefferson could easily guess why: when they learned of the proposed nomination, Federalists in the cabinet had threatened to resign *en masse*, and Adams was not willing to challenge them. Jefferson later recalled the street scene as the two old friends left the dinner. They came to Fifth Street "where our road separated, his being down Market Street, mine off along Fifth, and we took leave; and he never after that said one word to me on the subject or ever consulted me as to any measure of the government."

Adams had hoped to avoid the partisan conflict that had shattered the peace of Washington's last years, but Adams himself had doomed this hope by his decision to retain Washington's cabinet. Secretary of State Timothy Pickering, Secretary of the Treasury Oliver Wolcott, and Secretary of War James McHenry were fierce partisans of modest abilities, a choice of last resort for Washington after other nominees had turned him down. Worse yet, the trio were allies with Hamilton, and they looked to the New York lawyer, rather than the President, for guidance. The implications of Adams's decision were immediately apparent to Jefferson after his street-corner exchange with the President. The cabinet would do its best to keep the government on a collision course with France, perhaps even to the point of war. Shorn of influence in the administration, Jefferson hurried back to Monticello a few days later.

He was back in Philadelphia by May 11. President Adams had called a special session of Congress to deal with the French crisis. In what Republicans dubbed a "war message," Adams called on Congress to strengthen the nation's defenses on land

and on sea. His purpose, he said, was, not to prepare for war, but to win respect for a three-man commission that he planned to send to France to negotiate an end to the crisis. Congress instantly fell into a partisan wrangle, and Jefferson once again found himself at the eye of the political storm. He complained that he had become "the property of the newspapers, a fair target for every man's dirt." He really had little choice but to assume the role of party leader. Madison was in retirement, and leadership of Republicans in the House had devolved upon William Branch Giles, a pompous Virginian who could boast some oratorical skill and little else. Albert Gallatin, whose constituency was Republican western Pennsylvania, had already caught Jefferson's eye as a man who could handle the intricacies of public finance. Born in Geneva and educated in the spirit of the French Enlightenment, he was acquainted with the writings of Adam Smith and of Smith's intellectual forebears, the French rationalists who had coined the phrase *laissez faire*. Unfortunately for Jefferson's purposes, Gallatin in 1797 lacked national stature. Federalists and Republicans alike looked to Jefferson to speak for the opposition.

Much as he disliked controversy, Jefferson shouldered the party burden with a speed that to this day has astonished his biographers. Within the space of a month after his arrival in Philadelphia the bucolic master of Monticello had become an accomplished politician. He developed a wide circle of correspondents among Republican rank and file, urging them to maintain greater discipline in Congress. He resumed his earlier efforts to build up a party press, assisting new party organs and political pamphleteers like James Thomson Callender, who had fled Britain under indictment for sedition. Perhaps his most significant move was opening a correspondence with Aaron Burr. A conciliatory move was needed because Virginia Republicans, in order to ensure that Burr remained in second place, had thrown their vice presidential electoral ballots to Samuel Adams in 1796. Jefferson, no friend of Burr, probably regarded him as a necessary evil in the emerging party organization. Though Burr's reputation was somewhat unsavory, he had the most promising future of any Republican north of Pennsylvania. After describing the situation in the nation's capital as he saw it, Jefferson inquired about the prospects for New York. Burr gave a prompt and grateful reply, and a few days later he journeyed to Philadelphia. He was in the city when James Monroe—removed from his diplomatic post by Washington for being too pro-French—arrived from Paris. Burr joined Jefferson and Gallatin for a two-hour interview with the displaced envoy. Even though Madison was not present, the circle of Republican leadership was solidly in place by the time the special session of Congress ended in June 1797.

Not content with putting together a party apparatus, Jefferson that spring virtually made himself into what in Britain would be called a "shadow" president. Although he avoided the press, his correspondence made clear to Republicans what alternative policies he would pursue. Above all, he dreaded war because war would further divide the country, bring bloodshed to the frontier, ruin to the seaports, and crushing debt to the entire country. Jefferson instead would have avoided Adams's bluster and military preparations. He would have adopted a conciliatory tone toward France, assuaging French fears by explaining the true nature of Anglo-American relations. Britain, in Jefferson's view, remained the principal menace because its threat to American independence was economic. To Elbridge Gerry, perhaps the only man in the country who was still on good terms with both President and Vice President, Jefferson wrote:

> When we take notice that theirs is the workshop to which we go for all we want; that with them center either immediately or ultimately all the labors of our hands and lands; that to them belongs either openly or secretly the great mass of our navigation; . . . that they are advancing fast to a monopoly of our banks and public funds, and thereby placing our public finances under their control; . . . when all this, I say, is attended to, it is impossible for us to say we stand on independent ground, impossible for a free mind not to see and to groan under the bondage in which it is bound.

Gerry, significantly, was one of the three emissaries that Adams planned to send to France. It was important that he knew who the true enemy was.

Jefferson's return to Monticello that summer was not the usual flight to pastoral simplicity. Politics followed him home. Madison, Monroe, and Wilson Cary Nicholas, a newcomer to the inner circle, all went to the mountain that summer to confer on strategy. There was little to be done for the moment, however. Adams's nomination of a three-man commission had transferred the theater of negotiation to Paris. The delegation, while partisan, was better than Jefferson had expected. It consisted of Charles Cotesworth Pinckney, ensconced in the Netherlands after being rebuffed in Paris, Elbridge Gerry, and John Marshall. The latter was a Richmond attorney and a cousin of Jefferson's. Although his background and training were similar to his cousin's, Marshall had become a Federalist, a deviation that Jefferson attributed to his extensive speculation in western lands.

It would be nine months before the outcome of the negotiations in Paris would be known in the United States, and Jefferson was happy to exchange "the roar and tumult of bulls and bears" for the gentle conversation of his daughters and the prattle of his grandchildren. The social event of that winter was the marriage of his younger daughter Mary to John Wayles Eppes. Despite Jefferson's earlier concern that his daughters would bring "blockheads" into his household, Mary's choice of mate was as fortunate as Martha's. Eppes was elected to the House of Representatives in 1802 and attained a position of party leadership during Jefferson's presidency.

A BAD COLD AND UNCOMMONLY FOUL WEATHER, which rendered the rivers impassable, delayed Jefferson's return to Philadelphia at the end of 1797. He saw no reason to hurry, in any case, because there was little for Congress to do until the winds brought news from Paris as to whether there was to be peace or war. The two houses marked time with partisan bickering. Jefferson arrived on the twelfth of December and took up his customary lodging at Francis's Hotel, about three blocks from Congress Hall. Politics even governed social relationships by this second session of the Fifth Congress. A few weeks after his arrival Jefferson wrote to a friend: "Party animosities here have raised a wall of separation between those who differ in political sentiments." The American Philosophical Society offered the only relief from politics. Jefferson had been elected president of that body the previous spring and would remain in the office until 1815. Apart from the fellows of the Society, most of whom were Republicans, Jefferson associated only with political allies. Every day he boarded with a group of Republican senators and congressmen, whose conversation was almost exclusively political.

The Senate over which Jefferson presided, like the old House of Burgesses, had the atmosphere of a gentlemen's club. Although it numbered thirty-two, only about twenty or twenty-five attended on any given day. Each senator sat in a large red-upholstered chair with a desk in front of him. The vice president sat in a large, red, high-backed chair, slightly elevated, behind a mahogany table festooned with silk. An English visitor thought "the whole furniture and arrangements much superior to our House of Lords." The debates, which were not reported, were usually conducted with good decorum. Since Federalists outnumbered Republicans by about two to one, and utilized their majority to control all committees, there was little opportunity for partisan gambits.

The House of Representatives was more raucous and more evenly divided. Modern roll-call analysis indicates a total of 51 Republicans, 53 Federalists, and one independent if all members had been present on any given day. The fate of any partisan measure therefore depended on party discipline and attendance. With respect to the latter, Republicans were notoriously lax. William Branch Giles, on whom Republicans depended for leadership, did not take his seat until February 1798, citing as an excuse his recent marriage. He left for home mid-way through the spring, in company with three other lackadaisical Virginians. For much of that December to July session (the longest of any Congress to that time) Gallatin and a newly recruited lieutenant, John Nicholas of Virginia, were virtually the only spokesmen for the Republicans in the House.

The Republicans' poor attendance record may have reflected a general disgust with the quality of politics. Early in the session Connecticut Federalist Roger Griswold accused Vermont Republican Matthew Lyon of wearing a wooden sword during the Revolution. Lyon retaliated by spitting in Griswold's face, an insult that Griswold personally avenged on the floor of the House by beating Lyon with his cane. An unsuccessful Federalist attempt to expel Lyon occupied the House in debate for three weeks. Jefferson thought the whole affair degraded the general government. There is no evidence, however, that he personally sought to instill more discipline in his followers. In his letters to Madison, Monroe, and other friends, he sounded more like a reporter than a participant. He probably preferred to remain a party rallying point, leaving tactics to Gallatin and Nicholas.

The suspenseful waiting ended on March 4, 1798, when Secretary of State Pickering received a bundle of dispatches from the American commissioners in Paris. Although it required days to decode their contents, Pickering rushed to the President's house as soon as he gained a sense of their content. The next day Adams prepared Congress for the failure of the mission by sending it the most recent report from the envoys, indicating that the French government had refused to receive them. As Adams read more of the dispatches he learned that his envoys had not even seen the French foreign minister, Charles Maurice de Talleyrand-Pigord, who instead had negotiated through three private citizens (dubbed in the dispatches "X, Y, and Z"). These individuals, who turned out to be Swiss bankers, had demanded an apology from the American government for Adams's May 1797 address, a large loan to the French government, and a bribe to French officials—all as a condition for even opening negotiations. The governmental loan was the point at which the Americans balked, for it would have made the United States a nonbelligerent ally of France and undermined the Jay Treaty—all of which was precisely Talleyrand's purpose. The Americans indignantly rejected the demands; Marshall and Pinckney made plans to return home, while Gerry stayed on hoping for a French change of heart.

Adams's initial reaction was that the behavior of the French government required a declaration of war. However, he realized that Congress would not take that step without seeing the dispatches, and he feared release would endanger the envoys. Instead, on March 19, he sent a message to Congress asking for increases in the army and navy, fortification of harbors, the arming of merchant ships, and additional taxes to pay for these preparations. Republicans regarded the message as a declaration of war in all but name; Jefferson called it "insane." Suspecting that Adams had overreacted and was deliberately concealing the contents of the dispatches, Republicans demanded that Adams release the papers. Ultra Federalists, who had been alerted by Pickering as to the explosive contents of the dispatches, joined in setting the trap that Republicans had made for themselves. With a sigh of relief, Adams released the papers, and the country exploded in anger. A wave of patriotism swept outward from Philadelphia to the farthest reaches of the land. The toast of the day was "Millions for defense, but not one cent for tribute!" Republicans suffered by their association with France; Federalists basked in a popularity they had not known since the beginning of the Washington administration. Jefferson feared that the public outcry would "carry over to the war-party most of the waverers in the House of Representatives," giving the Federalists a strong majority to do as they pleased. (In fact, modern roll-call analysis indicates that no more than one or two "waverers" switched sides; Republicans reacted to the crisis instead with a difficult-to-explain absenteeism.)

Riding the crest of public outrage against France, Federalists pushed through Congress laws to raise new regiments of infantry, a large provisional army to defend against invasion, and additional warships for the navy. To administer the reborn navy (the Revolutionary navy had been dismantled), Congress created a Department of the Navy with a secretary of cabinet rank. It authorized the President to borrow additional funds, and it levied new taxes, including a direct tax on property, to be collected by the states. Although these measures looked to war, Federalists hung back from the final step, assuming that France would force the decision. Moreover, they could hardly act without a specific request from the President, and by mid-summer 1798 Adams was having his doubts.

The popular outcry was fading when on June 18 John Marshall landed in Philadelphia to a hero's welcome. Federalists in Congress seized the opportunity to print an additional 10,000 copies of the XYZ dispatches, an unprecedented number for a government publication. Under cover of the renewed enthusiasm for war thus generated, Federalists moved against their domestic enemies. In June and July 1798 Congress enacted a series of Alien and Sedition laws, aimed at suppressing the Jeffersonians leaders, intimidating their followers, and silencing their newspapers. The Federalist suspicion of aliens stemmed from the fact that many of the immigrants in the 1790s were political refugees from Britain, rebels fleeing from Ireland, and French planters escaping a slave uprising in Santo Domingo. All of these elements naturally drifted into the Republican Party, raising Federalist fears of the spread of international subversion, or Jacobinism.

The Naturalization Act raised from five to fourteen years the period required for citizenship, thus delaying the ability of immigrants to participate in politics. An Alien Enemies Act gave the President power to confine or banish aliens of an enemy country during a state of war. Republicans raised no serious objection to this statute, since its applicability depended on a declaration of war, and Jefferson did not bother to repeal it when he won the presidency. More vicious was an Alien Friends Act, which authorized the President to deport aliens that he deemed dangerous at any time. Because of the discretionary power given the President, Jefferson felt the measure flew "in the teeth of the Constitution" and was "worthy of the eighth or ninth century."

Federalists were not finished. In July Congress approved a Sedition Act which made it a federal crime to publish "any false, scandalous, and malicious" writings against the government, the Congress, or the President. Significantly absent from the protection of the law was the Vice President, who was left to defend himself against the slurs of the Federalist press. Sedition—libel or slander of the government—had been a common-law crime in

Britain for more than a century, and Parliament, fearing the spread of ideological contagion from France, had enshrined it in a statute in 1792. Federalists relaxed the common law somewhat by allowing truth to be offered as a defense. Republicans were unimpressed. It was almost impossible to prove the truth or falsity of a political opinion, and the statute assumed an authority that Congress lacked. Jefferson, who had never given much thought to the problem of free speech, conceded that states had the power to prosecute sedition. To him, the danger in the Sedition Law was its abuse of federal power.

By the time Adams signed the Alien Act into law most of the Frenchmen who were its target had fled American soil. Adams, who had not asked for the Alien and Sedition laws and thought them unnecessary, did not deport a single alien. The Sedition Act was another matter, in part because enforcement was left to Federalist prosecutors and judges. As to its real purpose, the clue was the provision by which it expired of itself on March 3, 1801. The Sedition Act was thus intended to silence, or at least intimidate, the Jeffersonian press during the presidential election campaign of 1800. In all, twenty-five newspaper editors (all Republicans) were arrested, seventeen indicted, and ten convicted. It hardly constituted a "reign of terror" in the French style, but neither was it the brightest hour for American civil liberties.

JEFFERSON FLED FROM THE POLITICAL DEMENTIA even before the Sedition Act was passed, arriving at Monticello on the third of July. Unable to trust the mails and needing time to think, he corresponded with no one for seven weeks, and when he commenced writing he relied on messengers, rather than the government post. He had always shunned controversy, and in this season of madness he found the time and wit to write an essay on Anglo-Saxon grammar. When the republican theorist John Taylor of Caroline wrote him to suggest that it was time to consider Virginia's secession from the Union, Jefferson replied: "A little patience, and we shall see the reign of witches pass over, their spells dissolved, and the people recovering their true sight, re-storing their government to its true principles."

Even so, he was certain that Federalists had overstepped the Constitution. The problem was what to do about it. It was widely assumed that the Supreme Court could review acts of Congress, though it had not yet declared one unconstitutional, but the Federalist complexion of the Court made it an unlikely ally. Instead, Jefferson decided to counteract arbitrary federal power by appealing to the sovereign states. Early in the fall he penned a series of resolutions intended for the North Carolina legislature and turned them over to his friend Wilson Cary Nicholas for disposition. Jefferson wanted the resolutions to appear to be the sentiment of a state; he did not want his authorship known (and indeed it was not known for many years). Nicholas was leery of North Carolina—perhaps because the parts of the state with heavy Scots and German populations were predominantly Feder-alist—and decided that Kentucky was more fertile ground for Jefferson's seed. He gave them to a friend who had recently emigrated to the western country for introduction to the Ken-tucky legislature. A week later Madison visited Monticello, saw a copy of Jefferson's resolutions, and decided to draft some of his own for adoption by the Virginia assembly.

The Virginia and Kentucky resolutions, adopted in Novem-ber and December 1798, represented the first extended state-ment of the doctrine of states rights. Adapting Lockean social contract theory to the American federation, Jefferson claimed that the Constitution was a compact among the states that delegated certain specific powers to a central authority. The federal government was only the agent of the states, set up to handle certain mutual problems, but the states retained ultimate sovereignty. Should the central government exceed its prescribed powers, the states had the right to intervene. Jefferson then went on to demonstrate that the Alien and Sedition laws were uncon-stitutional usurpations of power and declared that a "nullifica-tion" of them was "the rightful remedy." This was too stark a challenge to federal power for the Kentuckians, who deleted the term "nullification" before approving the resolutions.

Madison's resolutions, reflecting his judicious temperament, were more cautiously worded. They too were founded on the compact theory, but instead of using the word "nullify" (which invites the chaos of minority rule), Madison asserted the power of Virginia to "interpose" itself for the protection of its citizens against the arbitrary actions of the federal government. The Virginia and Kentucky resolutions were thus an early attempt to conceptualize the American federation, and as a theory of limited central government they provided the philosophical foundation for the Republican Party. But their immediate political impact was marginal. They did call attention to Federalist repression and occasioned considerable debate in several states, but not one state legislature responded favorably to the circularized resolutions. The Federalist legislation was ostensibly directed at aliens and subversives, and Americans seldom rally to the defense of those two elements. More important in undermining Federalist popularity was the impression of militarism conveyed by their efforts to enlarge the army and the burden of taxes necessitated by the war preparations. In the end, two factors finished the Federalists: Adams's statesmanlike efforts to end the undeclared war with France, which divided his party, and Jefferson's active—almost modern—campaign for the presidency in 1800.

WHILE THE KENTUCKY LEGISLATURE WAS LABORING over his resolutions, Jefferson returned to Philadelphia for the final session of the Fifth Congress. About the time Congress opened, Dr. James Logan, a Quaker Republican who had left the country the previous spring to sound out the true feelings of the French government, returned from his mission. Claiming to have contacted Talleyrand himself, Logan reported that the French earnestly desired peace. Federalists were outraged. The day that Jefferson took his seat in the Senate Federalist leaders introduced a bill to make it illegal for a private citizen to usurp executive authority by communicating with the government of a foreign state. At the time it was a petulant attack on the Republican Party and Jefferson himself, aimed at demonstrating that they were tools of France, but the Logan Act is still on the statute books.

Dr. Logan's report reinforced mounting evidence of a French change of heart. The belligerent response of the United States to the XYZ Affair had taken Talleyrand by surprise and no doubt weakened his position. The stance of the French government itself was weakened by the defeat of its navy at the Battle of the Nile and reverses on land that gave new life to Britain's coalition of monarchies. More important than Logan's news, so far as the President was concerned, was the return of Elbridge Gerry in October with news that Talleyrand was willing to resume talks in The Hague. Adams was becoming worried about the army that Congress had created. Washington had emerged from retirement to assume command, but Hamilton, whom Washington had insisted on being named second in command, was the real power. Adams was not sure of Hamilton's objectives, and he had begun to sense a public backlash to the Federalists' military preparations. "If this nation sees a great army to maintain, without an enemy to fight," he warned James McHenry, "there may arise an enthusiasm that seems to be little foreseen. At present there is no more prospect of seeing a French army here, than there is in Heaven." When Adams's son, John Quincy, chargé d'affaires in Berlin, reinforced what Gerry and Logan had reported, Adams made up his mind. In February 1799, without consulting his cabinet, Adams named Maryland Federalist William Vans Murray minister plenipotentiary to the French republic.

High Federalists were furious. Secretary of State Pickering called the projected mission "the most unfortunate and most humiliating event to the United States . . . since the commencement of the French Revolution." To appease Senate Federalists, Adams a week later added two more delegates to the commission, Chief Justice Oliver Ellsworth and William R. Davie of North Carolina. Jefferson ought to have been delighted at Adams's statesmanship, for he was risking his own political future by seeking to end a confrontation that had produced such rich benefits to his party. Jefferson, however, could not credit Adams's motives. He thought the nomination of Murray an attempt to parry the French overtures, in the expectation that Senate Feder-alists would scuttle the nomination. When Adams added to the delegation, Jefferson assumed the purpose was to delay the mission. The result in fact was delay, but the fault was not Adams's. The mission was sabotaged by Timothy Pickering, who delayed for months in drafting the instructions that would allow the commissioners to depart. In declaring himself for peace Adams had unwittingly exposed a gaping fissure in the Federalist Party as well as the warlike aims of his Federalist opponents.

EARLY IN 1799, WHILE CONGRESS DEBATED making further addi-tions to the army and navy, Jefferson began to turn his thoughts to the approaching presidential election. He wrote to Madison that the coming summer was "the season for systematic energies and sacrifices. The engine is the press. Every man must lay his purse and pen under contribution." He urged Madison to set aside a portion of every post day to write something for the newspapers and send it to him in Philadelphia. "When I go away I will let you know to whom you may send," he assured his friend, "so that your name shall be sacredly secret." Jefferson urged other Republicans to write for the press, and he gave secret encouragement and financial aid to newspaper editors and pam-phleteers, among them James Thomson Callender. Jefferson justified his aid to this literary renegade on grounds that he had suffered indictment under the Sedition Law. However, Callender's attacks on Adams were so abusive that Jefferson later denied encouraging him. Some of Jefferson's friends tried to warn him that Callender was not to be trusted, but he failed to heed the warning. Callender would repay him in 1802 by publishing the accusation that Jefferson had fathered the children of Sally Hemings, the slave girl who accompanied Polly to France in the 1780s. This legend, utterly without factual foundation, was kept alive by English travelers in the nineteenth century, who used it to titillate their readers, and the popular media occasionally repeats it to the present day.

Jefferson also aided in the distribution of political pamphlets favorable to the Republican cause. He sent a dozen such pamphlets to Monroe in February 1799, instructing his neighbor to give them to "the most influential characters among our countrymen" who might be able to sway their neighbors. He told Monroe to give them only to the uncommitted and not waste them on "persons already sound." Jefferson kept aloof from organizational efforts, however, leaving that to local initiative. In the spring of 1800 Virginia Republicans took advantage of the convening of the legislature to organize themselves on a statewide basis. They set up a central committee of five in Richmond headed by Philip Norborne Nicholas (older brother of Wilson Cary Nicholas), and a committee of the same number in each county. They also adopted an impressive ticket of presidential electors, drawn from all parts of the state, including such luminaries as George Wythe, Edmund Pendleton, and James Madison.

Ever alert for opportunities to spread his gospel, Jefferson saw an additional use for the organization. He sent Chairman Nicholas eight dozen copies of Thomas Cooper's *Political Arithmetic*, a pamphlet written in the spirit of Adam Smith, denouncing taxes and naval expenses and arguing in favor of international free trade. Jefferson asked the chairman to send a copy to each county committee. "Tho' I know that this is not the immediate object of your institution," he wrote, "yet I consider it as a most valuable object, to which the institution may be most usefully applied." He cautioned the chairman, however, to keep secret his own role in the business, lest his activities become a "handle" for his opponents. Jefferson, in short, engaged himself more actively in the presidential campaign in 1800 than any presidential candidate had ever been, and more actively, perhaps, than any presidential candidate in the first half-century of the republic.

Although election committees, like that of Virginia's, existed in several states, the Republican Party was far from being a national organization. It was rather a heterogeneous collection of regional, economic, and ethnic interests that had been neglected or alienated by the Federalist administrations. It had no clearly defined principles or objectives of its own. If the party was to succeed in 1800, Jefferson realized, it had to formulate a "platform" (the term was not yet in use) that would guide its adherents and widen its appeal. Jefferson utilized his correspondence with state leaders and with potential converts, like Elbridge Gerry, to articulate the Republican creed.

A letter to Gerry in early 1799 reflected this dual purpose. His fundamental principles were three. First, he declared that he was committed to preserving the Constitution "according to the true sense in which it was adopted by the States" and preventing the "monarchizing" of its features. By this he meant preserving the powers of the states against the central government, and within the central government preserving the power of the Congress against the President. He also favored a central government that was "rigorously frugal and simple, applying all the possible savings of the public revenue to the discharge of the national debt." Second, he wanted to protect freedom of press and religion and the right of the people to oppose and criticize the governing authorities. His third principle was to shy from the quarrels of Europe. "I am for free commerce with all nations," he told Gerry; "political connection with none, and with little or no diplomatic establishment." These principles, he thought, were unquestionably those of "the great body of our fellow citizens."

The letter had its intended effect. Within six months Gerry was a Republican candidate for governor of Massachusetts. Jefferson also expected letters such as this to circulate beyond the persons to whom they were addressed, and there is good evidence that they did so. Republican newspapers and party leaflets reflected the basic principles enunciated by Jefferson, and they spread his creed the length of the land. Republican publicists appealed to the small farmers and artisans of the North by stressing that the southern leadership of the party shared their involvement in productive labor, in contrast to the Federalist speculators and moneyed men who lived off the labor of others. Largely due to Jefferson's efforts and the organizational machinery that he inspired, the election of 1800 marked the dawn of modern electoral campaigning.

Federalists added a modern touch of their own to the election—mudslinging. Some historians have argued that the personal attacks on Jefferson in 1800 were the most vicious of any presidential campaign on record. Religion provided Federalists with their best ammunition. Pious New Englanders had long viewed Virginia as a land of idleness, debauchery, and irreligion. The Congregational clergy, who had a near-monopoly on the New England mind, scoured Jefferson's writings for evidence that he disbelieved in the Holy Scriptures and rejected the Christian religion. A Federalist clergyman in New York claimed that "the election of any man avowing the principles of Mr. Jefferson would . . . destroy religion, introduce immorality, and loosen all the bonds of society." Jefferson played into the hands of his critics by openly befriending the English scientist and religious nonconformist Joseph Priestley, who landed in Philadelphia in the mid-1790s with the specific intent of founding a Unitarian Church in America. English Unitarians were the fruit of rationalist seed of the Enlightenment; their name was derived from their supposed rejection of the Christian Trinity. Priestley's work, *The Corruptions of Christianity* (1782), which denied the Trinity, virgin birth, original sin, and the divine inspiration of Scripture, had deeply influenced Jefferson's thinking. Jefferson met Priestley for the first time in March 1797 when he traveled to Philadelphia for his inauguration as vice president. While he was in the city he attended a series of sermons that Priestley gave before his new Unitarian congregation. This, incidentally, was the only time on record that Jefferson contentedly and regularly attended church services. The two corresponded regularly on theological issues for years thereafter. The friendship between them was fuel for the Federalist fire.

Federalist attacks on Jefferson's supposed religious beliefs caused Republicans more discomfort than any other charge. Frantically they combed his *Notes on Virginia* seeking to demonstrate that his writings were actually favorable to Christianity. Jefferson never responded publicly to the calumny, but he did give his thoughts on the subject to Dr. Benjamin Rush. Writing on September 23, 1800, Jefferson told Rush that he believed that the "tribe of clergy" who were in arms against him were inspired by self-interest. He felt they wanted to impose on the country their own brand of religion and saw him as the chief barrier to such a move. Added Jefferson: "And they believe truly. For I have sworn upon the altar of god eternal hostility against every form of tyranny over the mind of man." The religious issue actually cut both ways in 1800. The dominant Congregational element in New England was staunchly Federalist, but dissenters in New England, notably the Baptists, were more inclined to vote for Jefferson, precisely because he stood for separation of church and state.

The central issue, nonetheless, was war or peace, and Adams's own statesmanship drove the fatal knife into the Federalist Party. Adams spent much of the summer of 1799 in Quincy, Massachusetts, attending a seriously ill Abigail. Pickering took advantage of his absence to delay further the drafting of instructions for the peace envoys, who waited helplessly at dockside. The annual yellow fever epidemic further disrupted the government, as officials scattered into the countryside. In October, Adams returned, found Pickering residing in Trenton and his peace commissioners still cooling their heels. In a burst of anger (not surprising for a man who had already yielded too often) Adams sent the commission off to France, and six months later he summarily dismissed both Pickering and War Secretary McHenry.

For once, the timing of an American peace commission was apt. While Ellsworth and Davie were at sea, Napoleon Bonaparte, France's most successful general, swept out the corrupt and inefficient government that had caused the decline of French fortunes in both Europe and America, and declared himself First Consul. Napoleon wanted peace with the United States because he was nursing ambitions for the recovery of the French empire in the New World, and when the American envoys landed in March 1800, he received them cordially.

Amid rumors of peace, Federalists could no longer maintain their military buildup. Washington's death in December 1799 doomed the provisional army; Congress began to dismantle it in February. Jefferson noted the change in atmosphere: "The rapid progress of public sentiment warns them of their danger, and they are passing laws to keep themselves in power," he wrote.

Jefferson was referring to a bill before Congress to expand the federal judiciary by establishing new courts and many new judges. The admission of new states since 1789 made some reform necessary, but the Federalist bill was flagrantly partisan, designed to make the judiciary a fortress against the rising tide of Jeffersonianism. By the narrowest of margins Republicans blocked the bill, but Federalists would be back with it in the lame-duck session that followed their electoral defeat.

There was no single "election day" in 1800. The states that provided for the popular choice of presidential electors balloted at various times in October and November. In nearly half the states presidential electors were chosen by the legislature. In those states the presidential outcome turned on a state legislative contest. The first and most crucial of these contests was in New York in May 1800. Because New England was Adams country and the South (except for South Carolina) overwhelmingly Jeffersonian, both sides regarded the middle states as crucial. New York itself was evenly divided, and control of the legislature depended on the contest in New York City. There Burr concentrated his efforts. He framed a ticket loaded with Revolutionary war heroes, and he met with total success. Republicans were swept into control of the assembly, and Jefferson was virtually assured of New York's electoral vote. Indeed, by Jefferson's own calculations, victory in New York would mean victory in the nation.

Congressional Republicans, who would meet in caucus to form the party ticket, as they had in 1796, recognized that the victory in New York earned Burr the nomination as Vice President. Caucusing in Philadelphia later that month, Republicans unanimously placed Burr on the ticket. Burr, still smarting from the party's failure to give him unanimous support in 1796, agreed to serve only after he was given assurances of perfect support from all Republican electors.

The Federalist caucus settled on Adams and Charles Cotesworth Pinckney, but the party was far from united. After Adams dismissed the Hamiltonians in his cabinet toward the end of May 1800 and replaced them with moderate Federalists (John

Marshall became Secretary of State), Hamilton launched a scheme to dump Adams. The plot turned on South Carolina, a state still under the nominal control of the rice planting gentry, but where Jefferson was widely popular. The idea was that South Carolina's presidential electors would cast one vote for Pinckney and one for Jefferson, thereby allowing Pinckney to outdistance Adams and, it was hoped, the Virginian as well.

At Monticello, Jefferson kept close tabs on the vote, which proved to be much closer than he had anticipated, even with New York in his pocket. Federalists showed surprising strength in Maryland, which divided its electoral vote five to five, and in North Carolina, which gave Adams four of its twelve electoral votes. In Pennsylvania, another battleground middle state, the legislature chose the presidential electors. Federalists controlled the upper house, Republicans the lower. Republicans tried to change the law to allow for popular selection of electors, but the Senate blocked this effort. As a result, Pennsylvania virtually cancelled itself, giving eight electoral votes to the Republicans and seven to the Federalists. At the end of November, by the time Jefferson departed for Washington, D.C., where the capital had been relocated, the contest depended on South Carolina. There Charles Pinckney, a staunch Republican despite being a cousin of the Federalist candidate, took command. The legislature was evenly divided: Charleston and its environs were Federalist, the up-country Jeffersonian. Pinckney coaxed and bargained a slim majority for the Republican electoral ticket and wrote breathlessly to Jefferson: "The election is just finished and we have (thanks to Heaven's goodness) carried it."

The final tally stood 73 electoral votes for Jefferson and Burr, 65 for Adams, 64 for Pinckney. (Adams men had turned the tables on Hamilton by tossing away one of their Pinckney ballots.) A better indication of popular feeling was the election for the House of Representatives, where Republicans won 67 out of 106 seats and thus a mandate for Jefferson's policies.

Both Jefferson and Madison quickly realized that somewhere a Republican vote had to be thrown away in order to prevent a tie between Jefferson and Burr, which would throw the election into the Federalist-dominated House of Representatives of the Fifth Congress. This was most easily done among their friends in the Virginia "college of electors," but the assurances given Burr at the beginning of the electoral contest caused Madison to demand a unanimous vote for Burr in Virginia. To achieve this he obtained assurances from an agent of Burr that votes would be thrown away from the New Yorker in other states. It never happened. When the results from far-off Georgia and Tennessee became known in early January, the election had produced a tie, seventy-three for each. In mid-December, before the final tally was known, Burr had publicly disavowed any notion that he "would be instrumental in counteracting the wishes and expectations of the people of the United States." As the possibility of a tie loomed his statements became more ambiguous, and by mid-January he had fallen silent. When the tie was announced Federalists instantly sensed an opportunity to preserve their influence in the government by promoting Burr over Jefferson when the balloting began in the House of Representatives. James A. Bayard, the lone representative from Delaware, informed Hamilton that "persons friendly to Mr. Burr" have "distinctly stated, that he is willing to consider the Federalists as his friends, and to accept the office of President as their gift."

Hamilton, to his credit, was not at all happy with this intrigue. He knew both Republicans well, having battled them for years, and he respected Jefferson's integrity, even though he disagreed with him in philosophy. Hamilton regarded Burr, on the other hand, as a dangerous schemer, "as true a Cataline as ever met in midnight conclave." Hamilton's sensible advice went unheeded, however, his intrigues against Adams in the election having cost him all credibility.

The House began balloting on February 16, just three weeks before the anticipated inauguration. The voting was by state, as required by the Constitution, and with sixteen states in the Union nine was the requisite majority. Jefferson received the votes of eight states, Burr seven, and one was divided. Through thirty-five ballots over the next week the division held firm. the impasse was broken when Bayard and other moderate Federalists, having received indirect assurances that Jefferson would not totally scrap the Federalist system, reversed their votes or cast blanks. Jefferson won by ten states to four for Burr, two divided. Jefferson was president, and Burr, though nominally vice president, was politically dead.

REFLECTING ON HIS ELECTION VICTORY from the platform of success, Jefferson discussed with his friend Joseph Priestley the fundamental differences between those who had rallied around his standard and those who had adhered to John Adams. The principal difference, he thought, was that his opponents looked "backwards not forwards, for improvement." Adams's model was the past, the precedents set by "our ancestors," and Adams had actually told his audiences that "we were never to expect to go beyond them in real science." In contrast, Jefferson felt that his election was a victory for the principle of change. "We can no longer say there is nothing new under the sun. For this whole chapter in the history of man is new. The great extent of our republic is new. Its sparse habitation is new. The mighty wave of public opinion which has rolled over it is new." A severance from the shackles of the past, a new era of freedom, freedom to pursue self-interest, freedom to believe as one wished and to express that belief publicly—that was the Jeffersonian vision, and that was the import of the election of 1800.

Chapter Six

---○---

The President as Liberal

AT NOON ON MARCH 4, 1801, the 57-year-old president-elect left his boardinghouse and walked over to the capitol where John Marshall, appointed chief justice by Adams only a few weeks earlier, was waiting to administer the oath of office. Only the north wing of the capitol had been completed, and it housed the Senate and Supreme Court. The south wing contained a temporary oval brick building, commonly called the "Oven," where the House of Representatives met in some peril to their lives, for the roof was unfinished and the walls were held up by scaffolding. As Jefferson mounted the steps to the Senate chamber, a company of Alexandria militia fired a salute. The procession was otherwise without pomp or ceremony as befitted the man and the occasion. A Washington lady caught the significance of the peaceful transfer of power. "The changes in administration," she noted in her diary, "which in every government and in every age have most generally been epochs of confusion, villainy, and bloodshed, in this our happy country take place without any species of distraction or disorder."

After taking the oath of office, the lanky Virginian, indistinguishable in dress or manner from the crowd below, rose to give his inaugural address. He had spent considerable time on the speech, revising it down to the last minute, and it was certainly one of his finest compositions. He was concerned first of all to allay the passions that had divided the nation for the past three

123

years and to reassure his worried opponents that he was no political fanatic. This he did by pointing out that Americans, whatever their party differences, were in agreement on fundamental principles. "We are all Republicans, we are all Federalists. If there be any among us who would wish to dissolve this Union or to change its republican form, let them stand undisturbed as monuments of the safety with which error of opinion may be tolerated where reason is left free to combat it." Amidst his reassurances Jefferson could not resist a gentle gibe at the Sedition Act.

He then addressed Federalist apprehensions about his political philosophy.

> I know, indeed, that some honest men fear that a republican government can not be strong, that this Government is not strong enough; but would the honest patriot, in the full tide of successful experiment, abandon a government which has so far kept us free and firm on the theoretic and visionary fear that this Government, the world's best hope, may by possibility want energy to preserve itself? I trust not. . . . Sometimes it is said that man can not be trusted with the government of himself. Can he, then, be trusted with the government of others? Or have we found angels in forms of kings to govern him? Let history answer this question.

Here indeed was a radical notion! Governments did not require for survival royal majesty and ministerial pomp, the support of armies and navies, or an alliance with the rich and wellborn. Government, suggested Jefferson, can be strong only when it has the affections of the people. And it can win those only by being attentive to the peoples' interests.

Jefferson's second concern was to outline his own political program. This proved to be a distillation of the platform he had developed through correspondence during the election campaign. It was, in essence, a statement—the first comprehensive one—of American Liberalism. "Equal and exact justice to all men, of whatever state or persuasion, religious or political; peace, commerce, and honest friendship with all nations, entangling alliances with none." Jefferson envisioned an evenhanded, unobtrusive government that would concern itself with protecting law and order at home and the peaceful pursuit of free trade abroad. This concept of political liberty easily blended with the economic liberalism expounded by Adam Smith in *The Wealth of Nations* (1776). Jefferson summarized it as "a wise and frugal Government, which shall restrain men from injuring one another, shall leave them otherwise free to regulate their own pursuits of industry and improvement, and shall not take from the mouth of labor the bread it has earned. This is the sum of good government." In Europe, where the message did not pass unnoticed, people could not believe that the chief magistrate of a country would voluntarily renounce patronage and power. It promised, said an English journalist, "a sort of Millennium in government."

Jefferson followed his inaugural reassurances with a refusal to dismiss Federalist officeholders. He announced that government servants appointed by Washington or Adams would be discharged only on proof of malfeasance in office. However, he made an exception for Federalists appointed by Adams after December 12, the day that Adams knew he had been defeated. The ex-president had in fact tried to pack the government with Federalists in his last hours. Jefferson regarded such appointments as "nullities" and therefore not chargeable as removals; he simply replaced them with Republicans. He also adopted a policy of naming only Republicans to fill vacancies in order to achieve a balance between the parties in officeholding. Even so, at the end of his first term Federalists still held almost half of the clerical offices in the federal service.

His policies generally reflected the same pragmatic moderation. Although several of his more ardent followers demanded constitutional amendments that would prevent a reenactment of the Federalist program of 1798, Jefferson saw no point in tilting with windmills. Most of the Alien and Sedition laws expired in 1801, and the new Congress quickly repealed the naturalization law. Jefferson had no intention of reinstituting such a policy, so amendments seemed unnecessary. The "reign of witches" was over, and the people had nothing to fear from him. Similarly, the

Federalist financial system, merchant-oriented though it was, had established the fiscal integrity of the government; to assault it head-on might disrupt the entire economy. Instead, he hoped to chip away at some of its more exposed edges. He retained the Bank of the United States, for instance, because it had been providing important services to the treasury, but he allowed Gallatin to sell the government's shares of stock.

Although the change in ruling elite from Federalists to Republicans hardly constituted the "revolution" that Jefferson later recalled, there was, nonetheless, a genuine shift in direction. Where Federalist ideology had stressed the depravity of man and the need for powerful rulers closely connected with institutionalized religion, Jefferson affirmed a faith in an enlightened populace that needed no overt guidance in matters political or religious. One measure of the difference was in their respective attitudes toward the civil service. John Adams believed in government by the wealthy, the wise, and the wellborn, and the men he appointed to office generally reflected these criteria. Jefferson felt that status and pedigree were no measure of worth; he looked only for men of talent and training. As a result, his choices began a gradual democratization of the governmental elite. The President's reach extended only to men, however. His attitude toward women in government had not changed since his proposal for all-male suffrage in the Virginia constitution of 1776. "The appointment of a woman to public office," he candidly told his Secretary of the Treasury, "is an innovation for which the public is not prepared, nor am I."

Jefferson did favor some changes in the law that would expand male suffrage and create a more equitable system of representation. Such reforms required state, rather than federal, action, however, and Jefferson had neither the temperament nor the will to interfere in local matters. His followers at the state level, moreover, evinced little interest in democratic progress. Even those "radicals" who demanded that every vestige of Federalism be purged from the government said nothing about universal white male suffrage. Though short on deeds in this regard, Jefferson spoke often of the virtue of the common man, and

Republican broadsides made frank appeals to him for support. Thus the Jeffersonian rhetoric alone enhanced the importance of the average citizen. Even the Federalists came to recognize that the common man was an integral part of the political process. As the parties competed for votes, they developed ever more sophisticated machinery for mobilizing the electorate. The result was a dramatic rise in voter turnout, reaching in some states as high as 80 percent of the eligibles on the eve of the War of 1812. This level of participation could be achieved only if the voters felt that the system was working, that it was responding to their needs. This was the triumph of Jefferson's rhetoric.

Jeffersonian democratization was, in part, a matter of image-making, and the President himself was a master at it. His own tastes were simple enough (except for his dinner table, which was always elegantly furnished), and he had little difficulty in creating an aura of republican simplicity. His predecessors' practice of addressing Congress in person appeared to him a vestige of monarchy. Since he was a wretched public speaker anyway, he initiated a practice of sending his messages to be read by the clerk of the House. The custom reemphasized the constitutional separation of executive and legislature, and was honored until the time of Woodrow Wilson. Jefferson also made himself accessible to all, though he was driven to distraction by the frequent interruptions of business. The studied effort to avoid European protocol even extended to Jefferson's dinner parties, where seating was pell-mell rather than by rank, a practice that offended the snobbish British Ambassador Anthony Merry.

Even the President's bowels became indirectly involved. He was much troubled by diarrhea at the outset of his term, and a doctor suggested horseback riding as a possible cure. Jefferson never had much faith in physicians, but he took the advice since he enjoyed riding anyway. His solitary rides around the federal district excited considerable attention, and observers compared his frugal habits with the ostentatious coach-and-six in which his predecessors had pranced around the capital city. Before long even his intestinal difficulties cleared up.

But there was substance, as well as imagery, in the concept of

Jeffersonian Democracy. His "wise and frugal government" contrasted sharply with the neo-mercantilism that had characterized Federalist economic policies. He desired a light-handed regime that neither burdened commerce with regulations nor the citizen with taxes. Labeling this concept "the politics of inclusion," some historians have argued that, without any elaborate theoretical foundation, it laid the basis for nineteenth-century liberal capitalism. Implementation of this ideal fell to the cabinet, notably Secretary of the Treasury Albert Gallatin.

LONG BEFORE THE ELECTION WAS OVER Jefferson had reached a verbal agreement with Madison that his friend would enter the administration as Secretary of State. Likewise, it was generally assumed that Gallatin would be named Secretary of the Treasury. However, Jefferson could make no public announcement of these appointments until after the election was decided by the House of Representatives. Jefferson then moved quickly to form his official family. The remaining appointments were dictated by the need for geographical representation, lest it appear to be a southern-dominated administration. General Henry Dearborn of Massachusetts became Secretary of War, and another New Englander, Levi Lincoln, became attorney general. Gideon Granger of Connecticut accepted the position of postmaster general, an office that had important patronage powers, though it was not at a cabinet level. The recently created position of Secretary of the Navy proved to be the most difficult to fill. After three men turned him down Jefferson quipped that he might have to advertise to fill the post. He won acceptance at last from Robert Smith, brother of powerful Maryland Senator Samuel Smith, and a Baltimore attorney with a large admiralty practice. Although Smith and the three New Englanders were overshadowed in the cabinet by the giant intellects of Madison and Gallatin, all four were capable administrators and, except for Smith, brought to their offices considerable political experience.

Jefferson believed that President Adams had allowed his department heads too much independent authority, and as a result the executive branch had drifted. In a Circular of November 1801 Jefferson told his cabinet that, while he had unqualified confidence in their abilities, he planned to be in control of his administration and in charge of its daily operation. Accordingly, he asked each department head to make up, once a day, "a packet of all their communications for the perusal of the President." In addition, Jefferson made himself available to members of the cabinet every day of the week, including Sunday. The proximity of government offices made frequent conferences possible. Flanking the president's mansion on the east was the brick treasury building, and another building to the west of the president's house contained the departments of state, war, and navy. Although the department heads usually waited upon the President, Jefferson occasionally visited them. In a typical note summoning his attorney general to a conference Jefferson wrote: "As soon as Mr. Gallatin comes to his office I have desired him to walk with me to Mr. Madison's office to consult on an important and pressing subject. Can you meet us there, and amuse yourself till Mr. Gallatin comes, the moment of which I am not able to fix." By maintaining an atmosphere of genial informality Jefferson kept himself informed of every detail of government and had a hand in the shaping of every policy decision. Jefferson decided against holding regularly scheduled cabinet meetings. He reserved such meetings for matters of some urgency. Formal meetings were usually held at noon so the business could be completed in time for the President to take his daily horseback ride before dinner at 3:30.

Jefferson's early dinner hour was an important part of the process of government. When Congress was in session, Jefferson invited its members to dinner, about a dozen at a time, on a schedule of three days a week. It was the President's principal social activity, as well as an important means of communication with Congress. Jefferson explained his motives thus:

> I cultivate personal intercourse with the members of the legislature that we may know one another and have opportunities of little explanations of circumstances, which, not understood, might produce jealousies and suspicions injurious to the pub-

lic interest, which is best promoted by harmony and mutual confidence among its functionaries. I depend much on the members for the local information necessary in local matters, as well as for the means of getting at public sentiment.

And the system worked. Few presidents have been as successful as Jefferson in having his every policy and principle enacted into law. In eight years in office, Jefferson never had occasion to use the presidential veto, while his successor Madison, who also had Republican majorities in Congress throughout his term, vetoed seven measures.

Entertainment on so large a scale entailed considerable expense and required good management. In August 1801 Jefferson employed Etienne Le Maire as his household manager, instructing him "that while I wish to have everything good in its kind, and handsome in style, I am a great enemy of waste and useless extravagance, and see them with real pain." Jefferson's French chef worked the kitchen under Le Maire's supervision, but Le Maire did the grocery shopping, every morning, in the Georgetown market. Jefferson himself oversaw the purchase of wines from Europe. Wine was a luxury that Jefferson could not do without. During his first term he spent $2,400 annually on wines, although he spent less in his second term when his cellar was well stocked. The cost of entertaining, the operation of his household, and the salaries of private secretary and household employees all came out of his annual salary of $25,000. In his first year his total expenses exceeded $33,000; thereafter he was able to live within his means. But he was not, while president, able to pay off any of the debts he had inherited from his father-in-law before the Revolution.

THE FISCAL POLICIES OF TREASURY SECRETARY Albert Gallatin were as central to the Jeffersonian system as Hamilton's had been to Federalism. Gallatin viewed a national debt as a curse, not a blessing, one to be dispelled as rapidly as possible. A businessman himself (he owned a glassworks and a gun factory in western Pennsylvania), Gallatin never thought of repudiating the debt Federalists had amassed. Instead he devised a program for retiring it over a period of sixteen years at the rate of $7 million a year. Gallatin estimated his annual receipts at only $9 million after the Federalists' internal taxes had been repealed, which meant that only $2 million would be available annually for the operation of the government. That meant cutting expenses and reducing the size of the federal payroll. The civil list could not be appreciably reduced, for Federalists had spent little money on officials and clerks. Indeed, the entire civil service resident in Washington, D.C. when Jefferson took office numbered only 127 persons. The best the Jeffersonians could do was to see to it that this did not increase, and in that they were successful. When Jefferson left office in 1809, despite having doubled the size of the country with the purchase of Louisiana, the federal bureaucracy in Washington numbered 123.

The military, on the other hand, was fair game. When the French crisis ended, Federalists had cut the navy even before they left office. An act signed by Adams on March 3, 1801, authorized the President to sell or take out of service all but six of the navy's frigates. Jefferson went even further, decommissioning all of the navy's ships, except for a small force that he sent to the Mediterranean to battle the Barbary pirates. In 1802 Congress fixed the army at one regiment of artillery, two regiments of infantry, and a corps of engineers, totaling 3,312 officers and men. Most of the army was scattered in frontier outposts. However, the corps of engineers was stationed at West Point, which became a military academy for the training of officers. The founding of a military academy might seem, at first blush, to run counter to Jefferson's oft-expressed hostility to the military. However, if there was one thing the Jeffersonians feared more than a standing army, it was a Federalist army. The evidence is scant, but it seems likely that West Point was designed to produce not only a professional officer corps, but one that was politically neutral.

These economy measures enabled Congress to repeal most of the Federalist excises; thereafter the government would subsist almost exclusively on the revenue from customs duties and the sale of public lands. In time, the delivery of mail was the only way many Americans would be aware that their government even existed.

The policies of Jefferson and Gallatin had a broader purpose than the goal of eliminating debt. In a note to Gallatin in 1802 Jefferson outlined the basic principle: "If we can prevent the government from wasting the labors of the people, under the pretense of taking care of them, they must become happy." A happy people, free of taxes and other restraints, would be a vital force in national development. Gallatin saw his fellow Americans, not as yeomen farmers, but as potential entrepreneurs. "Go into the interior of the country," he had told the House of Representatives in 1799, "and you will scarcely find a farmer who is not, in some degree a trader. In a grazing part of the country, you will find them buying and selling cattle; in other parts you will find them distillers, tanners, or brick-makers."

Some years later Gallatin described to Congress what he perceived to be the effect of the administration's fiscal policies. "No law exists here, directly or indirectly, confining man to a particular occupation or place," he exulted. "Industry is, in every effect, perfectly free and unfettered; every species of trade, commerce, art, profession, and manufacture being equally opened to all. . . . Hence the progress of America has not been confined to her agriculture." Adam Smith, with whose writings Gallatin was well acquainted, must have given a silent cheer from the grave, for this was a distillation of his Liberal thought.

Such a drastic reduction in the national debt in so short a time would disrupt a modern economy; that Jefferson and Gallatin got away with it is perhaps an indication of the lack of importance of the public sector in that day. Even so, they might have been in trouble but for the unparalleled economic boom occasioned by the war in Europe. After the French crisis ended, Americans were free to trade with both sides, and they expanded formerly illegal markets in the French and Spanish West Indies. American exports leaped from $56 million in 1802 to $95 million in 1805, and exceeded $100 million for the first time in 1806. Ultimately the neutral commerce would embroil the nation in the European war, but for the moment the proceeds relieved the chronic shortage of capital and financed a spurt of economic growth.

The customs receipts, in turn, exceeded Gallatin's expectations by several million dollars annually, enabling him to pay off the debt much faster than anticipated. Indeed, as early as 1806 Gallatin was faced with the prospect of an annual surplus. He went to the President with the problem, suggesting that perhaps the surplus could be invested in national development, a transportation network of roads and canals, for instance. Contrary to popular supposition, Liberal thinkers, such as Adam Smith, were not totally opposed to government activity. Indeed, Smith had conceded that there were a number of ways in which government intervention might be beneficial, with protective tariffs, for instance, or government investment in public works that furthered the nation's productivity. Jefferson also realized that a national prosperity dependent in large part on a war in Europe was a fragile one. Government investment in internal improvements would ensure a more stable future. The President therefore strongly endorsed Gallatin's idea, but he was unwilling to confine the investment to such mundane things as roads and canals. In his annual message to Congress the following January Jefferson called for an amendment to the Constitution to authorize the federal government to apply its resources to "the great objects of public education, roads, rivers, canals, and such other objects of public improvement as may be thought proper." Without waiting for Congress to act on an amendment, Gallatin prepared a plan for a national system of roads and canals. The only result, unfortunately, was the survey of a "national road" from Washington to Cumberland, Maryland, thence across the mountains to Wheeling, Virginia, on the Ohio River. Before anything more could be accomplished a succession of foreign crises that led eventually to war in 1812 blasted away Gallatin's surplus and eliminated any further thought of an investment in public works.

In their fiscal policies Jefferson and Gallatin departed in both theory and practice from the Federalist methods developed by Hamilton. But their innovations were tempered by an ideological flexibility about the role of government in the economy and a pragmatic awareness of political realities. A similar blend of democratic hopes, Liberal principles, and instinctive pragmatism characterized the other feature of the Jeffersonian "revolution"—the attack on the judiciary.

THE FEDERAL JUDICIAL SYSTEM, created by act of Congress in 1789, had become increasingly inadequate with the growth of population and the admission of new states in the 1790s. Special circuit judges were needed on the intermediate courts of appeal to relieve Supreme Court justices of the onerous duty of riding circuit. Additional district courts were required in the new states of the West. After Jefferson's electoral victory Federalists hurriedly passed a bill embodying these reforms so Adams would have the opportunity of making the new appointments before leaving office. The Judiciary Act of 1801 not only created a host of new circuit and district courts, as well as judicial offices for the District of Columbia, but it also reduced the number of Supreme Court judges from six to five upon death or retirement. This effectively prevented Jefferson from making an early appointment to the nation's highest court. Adams quickly set about making his nominations; indeed, rumor had it that he was up until midnight on the eve of the inauguration flooding the judiciary with Federalists. This lack of political sportsmanship shocked Jefferson, who feared that Federalists, having been defeated at the polls, were planning to turn the judiciary into a citadel to block his entire program.

Among the first measures of the Republican Congress was the repeal of the Federalist law, although their Judiciary Act of 1802 did retain a few of the lower courts in the western states. In the debate on this measure Federalists argued that the repeal violated the life tenure of judges guaranteed by the Constitution. Republicans responded that they were not dismissing judges, they were abolishing courts, and if a judge lost his job that was incidental. Federalists warned that the Supreme Court would find the new law unconstitutional, and Republicans answered by denying the power of judicial review. Relying on the Virginia and Kentucky resolutions, they argued that only states could review the constitutionality of acts of Congress. At this juncture John Marshall (himself a last-minute appointment, having been nominated to the post of chief justice in January 1801) intervened with his decision in the case of *Marbury v. Madison* (February 1803).

William Marbury was one of Adams's "midnight appointments," named a justice of the peace for the newly formed District of Columbia. But so late was the nomination made that James Madison found the undelivered commission on his desk when he took up his duties at the State Department. Under instructions from the President, who regarded the last-minute appointments as void, Madison refused to deliver the commission. Marbury promptly sued him, seeking a writ of *mandamus* (if issued, the court would command the official to do his duty and surrender the commission). To avoid delay Marbury instituted his suit in the Supreme Court, relying on a provision of the Judiciary Act of 1789 that gave the court original jurisdiction in cases involving a writ of *mandamus* against executive officials.

In deciding the case, John Marshall ruled that the court did have power to issue orders to executive officials, even when they were operating under the express instructions of the President. The only question in Marshall's mind was whether Marbury had followed the correct procedure. Article III of the Constitution listed the circumstances under which the Supreme Court could take original jurisdiction, but nowhere could he find any mention of the writ of *mandamus*. Marshall concluded that Congress had exceeded its authority by adding to the original jurisdiction of the court, and he declared that particular section of the Judiciary Act of 1789 unconstitutional. He therefore dismissed the case for lack of jurisdiction. Like many of Marshall's later decisions, the case was a political coup, for Marshall asserted a doctrine of judicial supremacy and let the Republicans win the case. Marbury never received his commission.

Despite his assertion of the power of a state to review the constitutionality of acts of Congress in the Kentucky resolutions, Jefferson was not opposed in principle to the doctrine of judicial

review. Although the Constitution is vague on the exact relationship between the courts and the other branches of government,
most lawyers accepted the concept in the 1790s. Jefferson himself had denied it only when faced with a partisan judiciary. His
objection to Marshall's decision focused instead on the *obiter
dictum* (words not necessary for the resolution of the case). After
dismissing the case for lack of jurisdiction, Marshall went on
unnecessarily to say what he would have done if he had jurisdiction. The chief justice upheld the power of courts to issue orders
to executive officials; even the president must be subject to the
law. This declaration confirmed Jefferson's suspicion that Federalists intended to use their judicial bastion to block everything he
wanted to do. Even so, Jefferson could not publicly object to
Marshall's *dictum* because to do so would have involved taking
the position that the president is above the law. This he could not
do, having inveighed against executive power throughout the
1790s. Thus Marshall's shrewdly calculated political gambit became a constitutional landmark. By declaring an act of Congress
void on the one hand, and establishing his authority over executive officers on the other, Marshall in one grand stroke promoted
the Supreme Court as the highest of the government's three
branches.

Chagrined, Republicans sought ways of cracking the Federalist hold on the judiciary. The contest between Congress and
the courts over the next two years seems in retrospect a sideshow
with little in the way of tangible result. While its exact political
effect is hard to gauge, the Republican assault on the judiciary
had potential appeal because courts and lawyers were never
popular in early America. The populace regarded them as agents
of the wealthy. Whether the matter at issue was a conflict over
land titles, a suit for debt, or a stray cow, the wealthy could better
afford to hire attorneys, transport witnesses, and impress juries.
Any decision reached by a court was then enforced with the full
powers of the government.

By 1803 the radical element in Jefferson's party was in full cry
against courts everywhere. The Pennsylvania assembly removed
one state judge who had openly flaunted his Federalism, and

then instituted impeachment proceedings against the entire supreme court of the state. In Congress various Republican leaders
were likewise discussing the use of impeachment as a means of
bringing the federal judiciary in tune with the new political
order. "We shall see who is master of the ship," said one. "Whether
men appointed for life or the immediate representatives of the
people . . . are to give laws to the community."

The procedure for removing officials was outlined in the
Constitution. The House of Representatives voted an impeachment (indictment), and the trial was conducted before the Senate, its members acting as judges. A vote of two-thirds of the
Senate was required for conviction and removal from office.
Unfortunately the procedure, when applied to judges, contained
a glaring loophole. The Constitution gave federal judges life
tenure during good behavior, but removal by impeachment required conviction for "Treason, Bribery, or other high Crimes and
Misdemeanors." And therein lay the gap. What if a judge misbe-
haved but could not be convicted of a crime? Or, put another
way, did the misuse of judicial authority constitute a misdemeanor within the meaning of the Constitution, or did the
indicted judge have to be convicted of a crime with due legal
process? William Branch Giles told the Senate that "impeachment is nothing more than an enquiry, by the two Houses of
Congress, whether the office of any public man might not be
better filled by another." Not all Republicans shared this radical
notion, however, and therein lay trouble.

The most inviting target for a test of the impeachment process was Supreme Court Justice Samuel Chase, a Maryland
lawyer who had switched from a near-fanatical opposition to the
Constitution to an equally fanatical Federalism once Washington
installed him on the Supreme Court. Because he was on the
court's southern circuit, he presided over the only sedition trial
held in Virginia in 1799–1800, that of James Thomson Callender,
the pamphleteer who had received secret financial assistance
from Jefferson. The state, "interposing" its authority pursuant to
Madison's resolutions, allowed its public attorney to aid in
Callender's defense. Chase conducted the trial in a grossly unfair

manner, publicly abusing Callender's attorneys and insulting the Commonwealth. His conduct in other sedition trials was equally injudicious; Republicans longed to get even.

Chase provided the occasion in May 1803 when he launched into a political tirade before a Baltimore grand jury. An angry listener clipped Chase's charge from a local newspaper and mailed it to Jefferson. The President reacted instantly. "You must have heard of the extraordinary charge of Chase to the Grand Jury at Baltimore," he wrote to Maryland congressman Joseph H. Nicholson, a Republican leader in the House and a brother-in-law of Gallatin's. "Ought this seditious and official attack on the principles of our Constitution, and on the proceedings of a State, to go unpunished?" Nicholson conferred with his close friends, House Speaker Nathaniel Macon and John Randolph, chair of the powerful Ways and Means Committee. A veteran of the congressional wars of 1798–1799, Randolph seized upon Jefferson's hint, and at the opening of Congress the following winter he moved that the House appoint a committee to investigate Chase's conduct. Randolph himself headed the seven-man committee that combed Chase's judicial career.

In the spring of 1804 the House approved eight articles of impeachment that had been drafted by Randolph. Randolph was a brilliant orator, who terrorized the House with a rapier wit and a razor-sharp tongue, but he was no lawyer. The allegations centered on Chase's highly partisan conduct on the bench, but the question remained whether his lack of judicial restraint constituted a crime.

The prosecution itself seemed uncertain when the trial opened before the Senate in February 1805. Nicholson argued that misbehavior was sufficient grounds for removal, and proof of a crime was unnecessary. Randolph followed with a rambling speech, the gist of which seemed to be that Chase was guilty of criminal misbehavior. The attorneys for the justice quickly pointed out that this allegation, in effect, required the Senate to assume the posture of a court of law. Hence a crime would have to be proved under the normal procedures of criminal law. The Senate agreed, and the judge was saved. Republicans failed to get the necessary two-thirds vote on any of the eight articles; they mustered a bare majority on only two.

Jefferson had told Nicholson in the letter that had initiated the whole episode that "it is better that I should not interfere," and there is no evidence that he did. Congress generated its own momentum; Jefferson neither commented on the proceedings nor tried to influence the outcome. He followed the hearings closely, keeping a tally sheet of the vote of each senator on each of the articles of impeachment, but he probably concluded that Randolph's eccentricity and the divisions within the party rendered the trial a lost cause. Although it ended in stalemate, the "war on the judiciary" was not without significance. Had Jefferson and Republican radicals like John Randolph had their way, the federal court system would have been seriously weakened. As it was, the judiciary retained its judicial powers and independence, but never again would it become the partisan tool of one political interest. Duly chastened, Republicans made no further attempts to impeach judges. There is perhaps no better evidence of Jefferson's own pragmatism, of his recognition, as he himself put it, "that no more good must be attempted than the nation can bear."

JEFFERSON HAD NEVER THOUGHT OF REFORM in a purely political context. He recognized that there existed many ways of improving society that did not require legislation, and he sought to use the influence of his office to that end. His service as president of the American Philosophical Society, although he did not preside over a meeting while president of the U.S., added prestige to scientific endeavor. He also maintained his previous practice of serving as a conduit for the ideas of others. At the suggestion of a Pennsylvania agriculturalist, he added an iron tip to the moldboard of his plow and then published a circular describing the function and advantages of the new device. Ever interested in agricultural improvements, he threw the weight of his office behind the idea of establishing a national board of agriculture modeled on the English board. The project was to unite local agricultural societies by having each elect a delegate to a national society in Washington. The national board began meeting in 1803 and elected Madison its president. Unfortunately a voluntary society, without government financial aid, lacked the power and influence of its English counterpart, but Jefferson could not bring himself to endorse public financing for such a project, useful though he thought it was.

Jefferson was willing to suspend the principle of nonintervention, however, where a specific scientific purpose could be shown. In 1801 Charles Willson Peale, artist and naturalist, was excavating the bones of a mastodon (known simply as a "mammoth" at the time) that had been discovered in a tar pit on a New York farm. Because the pit kept filling with water, Peale asked Jefferson for the loan of a pump from the navy. Jefferson quickly authorized the loan, and the skeleton was unearthed, taken to Philadelphia, and reconstructed in Peale's American Museum, where it attracted unusual attention. It was the first fossil skeleton mounted in America and only the second in the world.

The mastodon had long intrigued Jefferson because the animal appeared to be extinct in North America. Jefferson, like most disciples of the Enlightenment, believed in a "great chain of being," fixed by God at the Creation and no link of which could ever be lost. This concept viewed nature as a hierarchy of species, from the simplest plant to the highest animal, man. To Jefferson, the "economy of nature" required that, if the mastodon was extinct in North America, it must exist somewhere else. In a "Memoir on the Discovery of Certain Bones," a paper he had presented to the American Philosophical Society on assuming its presidency, Jefferson wrote that "the animal species which has once been put into a train of motion [the "chain of being"] is still probably moving in that train. For if one link in nature's chain might be lost, another and another might be lost, till this whole system of things would vanish piece-meal." For once in his life, reason betrayed him. He could understand nature only as a rational "system of things," and to adhere to this concept he had to ignore the physical evidence of the fossil record. There was, however, a final touch of irony to this story. In 1808, toward the

Jefferson's enthusiastic support of Charles Willson Peale's excavation of the fossilized mastodon demonstrated his willingness to use government in support of scientific research. The painting, *Exhumation of the Mastodon,* was done by Peale himself in 1806. *Courtesy of the Peale Museum, Baltimore.*

end of his presidency, Jefferson sent the bones of a mammoth to friends in France. Examination of these bones, and comparison with European fossils, led European scientists to conclude that extinction was an established fact. This realization was the first step in the development of the theory of evolution, which replaced the concept of the "chain of being" in the course of the nineteenth century.

While Jefferson recognized the limits of his power in the pursuit of science, in another area, the design of the federal city, his authority was clear and the responsibility cheerfully accepted. When the government moved to Washington in the winter of 1800–1801, L'Enfant's grand vision was still mostly a blueprint. Both the capitol and the president's house were unfinished, and Pennsylvania Avenue, which connected the two, was little more than a woodland path on which congressmen sometimes got lost when returning to their lodgings after dining with the President. Although the north wing of the capitol, where the Senate sat, had been completed, it was almost immediately in need of repair. The south wing consisted of temporary partitions that barely kept out the wind. Representatives grumbled constantly and annually entertained a bill to remove the government to Baltimore or Philadelphia.

On taking office Jefferson directed the commissioners for the District of Columbia to give priority to two projects. First, he wanted a good roadway constructed from Georgetown down Pennsylvania and New Jersey Avenues to the Eastern Branch of the Potomac, a distance of about four miles. By 1804 Pennsylvania Avenue had the appearance of the boulevard that Jefferson had planned, lined with trees, with gutters and footpaths shaded by a second row of trees. The trees were Lombardy poplars, a favorite of his, although he loved all trees and planted many species at Monticello. (Margaret Bayard Smith, who kept a diary of her experiences in Washington as the wife of the city's most prominent newspaper editor, recorded a delightful conversation with Jefferson on trees. Jefferson had exclaimed, "How I wish that I possessed the power of a despot!" When she showed surprise, he went on, "Yes, I wish I was a despot that I might save the noble and beautiful trees that are daily falling sacrifice to the cupidity of their owners, or the necessity of the poor," who cut them for firewood.)

Jefferson's second priority was the completion of the south wing of the capitol. William Thornton's original design had been Roman in style, and that had been followed in the north, or Senate, wing. Although he realized that the south wing had to match the north in style, Jefferson was determined to find the best architect/engineer in the country to finish the job. In March 1803, after Congress appropriated $50,000 for the public buildings, Jefferson appointed Benjamin H. Latrobe as capitol architect. Born and trained in England, Latrobe moved to Virginia in

1796 where he completed the facade on Jefferson's state house. Jefferson met him in Philadelphia a year later when he was designing the building for the Bank of the United States, the first Greek Revival structure in America. Although Latrobe preferred Greek forms, while Jefferson's taste leaned to the Roman, they cooperated on completing the capitol with only minor disagreements. (Jefferson even approved of Latrobe's use of corn cob capitals on the columns of the south wing, which generally met derision from foreign travelers.) By the time Jefferson left office the capitol had taken on its present form, except for the modest Roman dome, which was replaced by the present massive structure in the mid-nineteenth century.

WHILE LIBERALISM WAS THE GUIDING SPIRIT of Jefferson's domestic policy, nationalism was the central principle of his foreign policy. Nationalism in the realm of foreign affairs took two forms—it involved a sensitivity to the nation's honor and prestige abroad, and, secondly, it fostered an aggressive expansion of American territory. The first was evident in the American resistance to British transgressions on the high seas that began during Jefferson's second term and culminated in the War of 1812 under his successor. But Jefferson also revealed a sensitivity to national honor at the very beginning of his presidency when he found himself at war with pirates in the Mediterranean.

The Muslim city-states along the Barbary Coast of North Africa (Algiers, Tunis, Tripoli) made their living by preying on the commerce of the Mediterranean. Through the latter half of the eighteenth century every major seafaring nation paid them an annual tribute to avoid having its commerce plundered. After Independence, the American government adopted the same policy, although the Washington administration had begun constructing warships in 1794 when the pirates threatened to emerge from the Straits of Gibraltar and begin preying on the commerce of the Atlantic.

When the pasha of Tripoli, dissatisfied with the amount of tribute he was receiving, declared war on American commerce in

May 1801, Jefferson summoned his cabinet and put the question: "Shall the squadron now at Norfolk be ordered to cruise the Mediterranean?" And, if so, "what shall be the object of the cruise?" For the second time in three years the nation found itself on the edge of a fight without a declaration of war by Congress. The question was how far the president's power extended when it came to taking military action on his own authority. The cabinet decided that the cruise should be undertaken and that American ship captains could be authorized to search for and destroy enemy vessels. This conclusion revealed Jefferson's willingness to use executive power, especially when the issue was the country's honor abroad.

In reporting the decision to Congress, Jefferson emphasized the defensive nature of the mission. Nevertheless, having decided to commit the navy, he prosecuted the war with vigor. Several of the navy's frigates were put back into commission, and by 1803 a squadron commanded by Commodore Edward Preble was blockading the harbor of Tripoli. The pasha eventually realized that the war was costing him his normal sources of revenue through piracy and ransom, and in June 1805 he signed a peace agreement.

Jefferson viewed the result with understandable pride. When Commodore Preble negotiated similar treaties with Algiers and Tunis, the United States, alone among the major commercial nations of the world, could traffic in the Mediterranean without harassment or tribute. Though unintended by Jefferson, the conflict also provided both training and tradition for the young navy. When the nation again went to war, in 1812, it would give a good account of itself. The Barbary War and the Louisiana Purchase, which reflected the expansionist element of Jeffersonian nationalism, were the great triumphs of his foreign policy.

SPAIN'S POSSESSION OF THE GULF COAST and the mouth of the Mississippi was an obstacle to American expansion, but the nation's initial interest in the region was not simply a matter of land hunger. Instead, it was essentially commercial. Every river of the lower South flowed through Spanish territory before emptying into the Gulf of Mexico, and the rest of the trans-Appalachian West was dependent on the Mississippi River for access to world markets. Throughout the 1780s and 1790s the American West had simmered with discontent at the Spanish stranglehold, alternating between plots to seize New Orleans by force and schemes of secession and independence. In 1795 President Washington temporarily placated the West by winning an agreement from Spain to open the lower Mississippi and the port of New Orleans to American commerce. After the river was opened, New Orleans handled more than a third of all American exports, a measure of the commercial stakes involved.

Despite its strategic advantage, Spain was not comfortable. The revenue from Louisiana and Florida never equaled the costs of administration. The region's only value to Spain was that it served as a buffer between the expansive United States and Spanish Mexico. By 1800 Spain was firmly allied to France, and French control of the region offered the prospect of an even stronger buffer. Napoleon, in turn, dreamt of recreating the New World empire that France had lost in 1763, and a deal was quickly consummated. By the Treaty of San Ildefonso, Napoleon promised the throne of Italy to the brother-in-law of the Spanish king and received in return an empire that included the mouth of the Mississippi and the entire basin from the river west to the Continental Divide. Anticipating an adverse American reaction to the presence of a powerful and militant neighbor on its western border, the two European powers agreed to keep the treaty secret. Spanish officials continued to administer New Orleans, and they kept the port open to American traders.

Within a year the swap was common knowledge among diplomats in Europe, and Jefferson learned of the treaty shortly after his inauguration. His reaction was restrained since for the moment there was no overt threat to American interests. His new minister to France, Robert R. Livingston, was instructed only to seek assurances for continued American use of the Mississippi. Madison later asked him to determine whether the French might be willing to sell New Orleans and the Gulf Coast, but Livingston was unable to find out from Talleyrand whether West Florida (the coastline south of the Thirty-first Parallel extending from the Perdido River west to the Mississippi) was even included in the Spanish cession.

In the spring of 1802, Jefferson decided to turn the screws. He informed Livingston, in an open letter sent by way of a friend, "There is on the globe one single spot, the possessor of which is our natural and habitual enemy," he wrote. "It is New Orleans. . . . France placing herself in that door assumes to us the attitude of defiance." Knowing that French officials would see the letter, Jefferson warned that a French takeover of New Orleans would trigger an alliance between the United States and Great Britain. This was more bluster than policy, but it did reveal Jefferson's single-minded pursuit of American national interests.

As it turned out, Jefferson did not have to carry out his threat of playing one European power off against the other, for within a year Napoleon's imperial plans were dead, stung to death by a mosquito. In 1802 Napoleon sent a magnificent army of 30,000 to occupy and hold Louisiana, but he ordered it first to stop in Santo Domingo and suppress the slave rebellion that had broken out on the island some years before. The army never got any farther. It was decimated by yellow fever; by September 1802 it was reduced to 4,000 effective soldiers and its commander was dead. When he learned of the disaster, Napoleon realized that it would be impossible to occupy New Orleans and hold it against an Anglo-American attack. Moreover, he anticipated a renewal of the war in Europe, and in that event New Orleans was a hostage to the British navy. In chronic need of funds to feed his war machine, Napoleon decided to sell his New World real estate to the Americans.

In the meantime, in October 1802, anticipating the arrival of the French, Spanish authorities in New Orleans closed the port to American shipping. War fever swept across the West, and Congress entertained resolutions that would authorize the President to seize New Orleans. To allay the war sentiment and put new pressure on the French, Jefferson sent to Paris his Virginia colleague James Monroe, known as a friend to France. Monroe was instructed to purchase New Orleans and West Florida, paying no more than $10 million, or at least secure the use of the Mississippi if Napoleon proved unwilling to sell out. Failing both, he was to journey to London and sign a defensive alliance with the British. By the time Monroe reached Paris in April 1803, Napoleon had made an offer of sale to Livingston. Monroe quickly joined in the negotiations, and the treaty, signed in May, gave the United States New Orleans and the Louisiana Territory, from the Mississippi River to the Rocky Mountains, for $15 million.

Despite the fact that the American commissioners had exceeded their instructions (told to buy the Gulf Coast, they also bought the Great Plains and paid 50 percent more than authorized), Jefferson was delighted with a purchase that doubled the size of the nation and gave the United States control of both the Mississippi and Missouri rivers. He had long felt that it was the destiny of the American republic to overspread the continent. Shortly after the Revolution he had told a fellow Virginian: "Our confederacy must be viewed as the nest from which all America, North & South is to be peopled." Referring to the purchase as an "empire for liberty," Jefferson told Congress that the acquisition offered "an ample provision for our posterity, and a widespread field for the blessings of freedom and equal laws." Jefferson was clearly referring only to white posterity, for the acquisition also offered a vast field for the expansion of slavery. The institution already existed in New Orleans and the settled areas around it, and the treaty guaranteed the residents of Louisiana all the rights of citizens of the United States. Nevertheless, given his earlier opposition to the expansion of slavery, Jefferson might have been expected to support a restriction of slavery in the remainder of the purchase. He did not. When in 1804 a New England senator offered an amendment to the bill organizing the Orleans territory that would have prohibited slavery in the entire purchase, Jefferson ignored it. The most that either Congress or the President would support was a prohibition on the further import of slaves into Louisiana from abroad.

Jefferson was more concerned, in fact, about the legality of the purchase. A quick check of the Constitution revealed that there was indeed no delegated power that authorized the federal government to purchase an empire. Wishing to avoid setting a precedent for an elastic construction of the Constitution, Jefferson drafted an amendment that would retroactively legalize the purchase. Cabinet members dissuaded him, however, pointing out that there were no limitations on the government's treaty-making power under the Constitution. In the Senate the principal opposition came from Federalists who feared the further dilution of New England influence and demanded that Louisiana be kept permanently in a colonial status. The Senate ratified the treaty by a vote of 24 to 7, with only one Federalist deserting ranks to support the acquisition.

The ex-president's son, John Quincy Adams, newly elected by the Massachusetts legislature, favored the purchase, but he arrived in Washington too late to vote on the treaty. Adams, however, alone among senators, thought the acquisition of Louisiana required a constitutional amendment. Years later he complained that the purchase of Louisiana was "an assumption of implied power greater in itself and more comprehensive in its consequences than all the assumptions of implied powers in the years of the Washington and Adams Administrations put together." The purchase, it is fair to note, did fly in the face of the doctrines of strict construction and states rights, enunciated in the Virginia and Kentucky resolutions. Jefferson simply found that the responsibilities of power required him to be flexible and pragmatic; only those out of power can afford the luxury of dogmatic consistency.

Jefferson had long wondered what mysteries lay in the vast land mass between the Mississippi River and the Pacific Ocean. Mountains? Deserts? Trackless forests? Unknown species of plants and animals? In November 1802 Jefferson inquired of the Marques de Casa Yrujo, the Spanish minister in Washington, if his government would object if the United States sent an expedition to explore the course of the Missouri River, with the principal objective being to advance knowledge of the geography of the continent. The minister replied that such an expedition "could not fail to give umbrage" to his government, but he relayed the request to his superiors in Madrid.

Despite Spanish resistance and the pending transfer of Louisiana to France, Jefferson pressed ahead with his plan. In January 1803 he asked Congress for an appropriation of $2,500 to finance the expedition. Recognizing that Congress had no constitutional authority to appropriate money for "a purely literary expedition," Jefferson explained that the object was to find "the most direct and practicable water communication across this continent, for the purposes of commerce." Congress quietly appropriated the funds. Jefferson had already chosen a commander, his Albemarle neighbor and private secretary, Meriwether Lewis. Although only twenty-eight years old, Lewis had extensive knowledge of the western country. Lewis was made a captain in the army, and, on a promise of joint command, he obtained the services of another army officer, William Clark, younger brother of Revolutionary war hero George Rogers Clark.

By the time he drafted instructions for Lewis and Clark in June 1803, Jefferson was aware that the French had offered to sell Louisiana, though he had not yet received word of the signing of the treaty. It was another year before the expedition, recruited mostly from the ranks of the army, set forth upriver from St. Louis. And it would be two more years before it returned with priceless scientific and geographic information about the interior of the continent.

JEFFERSON WAS STILL BASKING IN THE WARMTH of popular approval of the Louisiana Purchase when he stood for re-election in the fall of 1804. Republicans had amended the Constitution to prevent any recurrence of the Federalist attempt to abort the popular will, such as had occurred in the last contest. The Twelfth Amendment required separate ballots for president and vice president in the electoral college, in effect writing into the Constitution the concept of a party ticket. In May 1804 Republican members of Congress met in caucus and unanimously renominated Jefferson for president. With equal unanimity they dropped Burr from the ticket, handing the vice presidential slot instead to Burr's rival in New York politics, elderly Governor George Clinton.

Burr's political fortunes had declined steadily after the electoral contest in the House in 1801. In his first year in office, Jefferson had pointedly ignored Burr's patronage recommendations for New York and named instead allies of the Clinton and Livingston clans. By 1804 Burr's support in New York had eroded to the point that Republicans refused to nominate him for governor. Burr ran anyway, hoping to attract Federalist support. He lost, blamed the defeat on Hamilton's intervention, and mortally wounded Hamilton in a duel. Wanted for murder thereafter in both New York and New Jersey (where the duel was fought), Burr was finished as a politician.

The result of the election was never in doubt. Jefferson's record, capped by the Louisiana Purchase, was one of extraordinary achievement, both domestically and abroad. Republicans carried all but two states, Connecticut and Delaware. The electoral vote was 162 for Jefferson to 14 for Charles Cotesworth Pinckney, the Federalist candidate. Republicans also made extraordinary gains in Congress, reducing the Federalist component in the House of Representatives to fewer than thirty.

Storm clouds nevertheless loomed on the horizon. The United States had profited by the rivalry of Britain, France, and Spain in Jefferson's first term. But the fighting in Europe intensified during his second term. Napoleon crowned himself emperor of France in 1804, and Britain organized a Third Coalition of monarchies (Austria, Russia, and Sweden) to check his ambitions. The war would soon become a death struggle between Britain and France, and the neutral United States would be caught in the middle. Jefferson struggled vainly to uphold America's honor and interests, but the hounds of war overpowered him in the end.

Chapter Seven

○

The President as Nationalist

THE SENATE ACQUITTED SUPREME COURT Justice Samuel Chase on the impeachment charges leveled by the House of Representatives on March 1, 1805, just three days before Jefferson was sworn in for his second term. It was an inauspicious beginning, for the Chase trial had fractured the Republican Party. John Randolph of Roanoke, who almost single-handedly had masterminded the attack on Chase, blamed the President and, more particularly, Secretary of State Madison, for the failure to remove Chase. Randolph had become increasingly discontented with Jefferson's compromises, in particular his failure to purge Federalists from the government. A doctrinaire relic of the party battles of the 1790s, Randolph was offended by Jefferson's use of executive authority and suspicious of Jefferson's influence over Congress. Bitter and vindictive, temperamentally unstable and suffering from chronic internal disorders, Randolph would have been of no consequence, but for one aspect—he was on intimate terms with the House leadership, notably Speaker Nathaniel Macon and the speaker's lieutenant, Joseph H. Nicholson, who served on more committees than any other member. A confrontation with Spain at the outset of Jefferson's second term gave Randolph an opportunity to cause trouble.

The dispute between the United States and Spain over West Florida originated in the undefined boundaries of Louisiana. The treaty defined the purchase as "Louisiana with the same extent as it now has in the hands of Spain, and that it had when France possessed it." Unfortunately, these were two different things. Louisiana as a French possession embraced the whole Mississippi valley, from the Appalachians to the Rockies, and thus included West Florida. However, West Florida, along with the rest of Louisiana east of the Mississippi, went to Britain in 1763, and Spain got control of it only in 1783 when Britain was forced to cede both East and West Florida by the treaty that ended the American Revolution. The question was: did Spain cede West Florida to France in 1800, and, if so did the United States purchase it in 1803?

The question was important, for the Gulf Coast, which held the commercial key to the American South, was more valuable at the time than the whole expanse of grassland west of the Mississippi. Monroe and Livingston were both in France with orders to buy it if possible, and they naturally asked foreign minister Talleyrand if West Florida was included in the Louisiana deal. Talleyrand, who felt France benefited by having the United States and Spain at odds with one another, replied enigmatically: "Gentlemen, you have made a noble bargain for yourselves, and I suppose you will make the most of it." Taking the hint, Monroe and Livingston informed the President that they considered West Florida part of the Louisiana Purchase. Jefferson and Madison agreed, and it became official policy that West Florida was American soil, although they refrained from occupying it.

Seemingly surrounded by duplicity, Spain reacted angrily. The Spanish regarded the Louisiana Purchase as illegal, since their agreement with Napoleon had stipulated that it was not to be sold, and they had no intention of surrendering West Florida. Encouraged by the French, they began plundering American commerce on the high seas. Periodic gunfights on both the Texas and Florida borders punctuated the deterioration of Spanish–American relations. In late 1804 Monroe, who had been made minister to Great Britain, journeyed to Madrid in search of a settlement of the boundary dispute. Stopping in Paris on the way, he learned that the French had reversed themselves on the question of West Florida. That doomed any chance of success in

Spain because Napoleon totally dominated his weak neighbor. After five frustrating months in the Spanish capital, Monroe gave up and returned to London.

Jefferson learned of the failure of Monroe's mission in August 1805, while at Monticello, and he correctly blamed France for the setback. By the time he returned to Washington in October Jefferson had concluded that West Florida could be acquired only by purchase and that the negotiations had to be held in Paris. He told Madison that with "France as the mediator, the price of the Floridas as the means. We need not care who gets that [i.e. the payment]: and an enlargement of the sum we had thought of may be the bait to France." Jefferson the idealist had become the artful practitioner of *realpolitik*.

On November 12, three weeks before Jefferson was to present his annual message to Congress, the cabinet adopted Jefferson's plan of purchasing both Floridas, while making concessions to Spain with respect to the border between Louisiana and Texas. In a memorandum of the meeting Jefferson noted that American money would be "the exciting motive with France, to whom Spain is in arrears for subsidies, and who will be glad also to secure us from going into the scale with England." As chance would have it, the very next day dispatches arrived from John Armstrong, who had replaced Livingston in Paris, outlining a plan for resolving the boundary controversies. If the United States, Talleyrand had suggested, would submit its dispute with Spain to Napoleon for arbitration, he would induce his Spanish ally to part with West Florida and a portion of Texas for $10 million. The sum coincided with the amount which Spain annually paid to France as a war subsidy. and it was clear that the money would wind up in French coffers. Armstrong noted that French speculators in American securities were already swarming around the foreign office.

Unconcerned that Napoleon was beginning to make a habit of selling Spanish real estate, Jefferson quickly summoned the cabinet. Talleyrand's proposal dovetailed nicely with the policy already approved by the cabinet, except for the sale price, which the cabinet reduced to $5 million. A congressional appropriation was necessary, and the cabinet decided to ask for a downpayment of $2 million. Because both secrecy and speed were essential, Jefferson and Madison devised a plan that was both ingenious and disingenuous. In his annual message the President sounded a highly belligerent tone, reviewing the difficulties with Spain and requesting additional troops. This was for both domestic and foreign consumption, but the President was quite serious. On that same day he wrote to Andrew Jackson, commander of the Tennessee militia: "Whensoever hostile aggressions . . . require resort to war, we must meet our duty and convince the world that we are just friends and brave enemies." Three days later he informed Congress secretly that the whole matter could be settled peacefully if the administration were given the means. When John Randolph, chair of the Ways and Means Committee, called on the President to get the details, he was told that the administration needed $2 million as a starter.

Randolph flatly refused to participate in any such underhanded scheme. To him the whole arrangement had the unsavory aroma of the XYZ Affair; it smacked of speculative Federalist chicanery. Already displeased with Jefferson's compromises, Randolph viewed this plot as final evidence that the President had lost his republican principles. In addition, Randolph had become suspicious of executive influence in Congress, and he particularly disliked a scheme in which the President could take the high ground publicly, while secretly asking the Congress to engage in bribery. He broke with the President and caused the first serious rift in the ranks of the Republican Party.

No more than a dozen southern Republicans sided with Randolph. Administration ranks generally held firm, and the Two Million Act passed in the spring of 1806. The delay occasioned by Randolph's opposition, however, doomed for the moment the effort to acquire West Florida. By the time Congress appropriated the money, Napoleon had departed for a campaign in central Europe and had lost all interest in Florida. The real damage from the schism was to Jefferson's prestige. To that point the President had seemed invincible. Randolph's accusations rattled the confidence of Republicans and sowed seeds of suspicion, not only in Congress but in crucial Republican states, like Virginia, Pennsylvania, and New York. For the remainder of his term Jefferson could not count on getting what he wanted from Congress; he often had to cut a bargain and make concessions in order to turn a policy into law.

JEFFERSON WAS ALSO LOSING SOME of his bargaining power abroad in the winter of 1805–1806. Lord Nelson's victory over the combined French and Spanish fleets in the Battle of Trafalgar in October 1805 forestalled a French invasion of the British Isles and left Britain supreme on the high seas. The following December Napoleon won a major victory at Austerlitz that doomed Britain's imperial coalition. "What an awful spectacle does the world exhibit at this instant," Jefferson wrote in January 1806, "one man bestriding the continent of Europe like a Colossus, and another roaming unbridled on the ocean. But even this is better than that one should rule both elements."

Even the bright side that Jefferson saw had its perils, for in truth the division made the position of the United States increasingly difficult. Britain could do what it wished with American shipping and seamen on the Atlantic with little risk to itself, and Napoleon had no need for American friendship or support on the Continent. The threat to play one belligerent off against the other, Jefferson's trump card in his first term, had all but vanished. Moreover, since neither of the belligerents could engage the other militarily, the war turned into a gigantic economic squeeze, as each tried to demolish the trade of the other. Caught in the middle was the neutral United States, helplessly watching its ships seized by both sides.

Although Napoleon seized as many American vessels as the British did, Americans directed most of their wrath against Britain. Most French seizures occurred in French ports, while Britain interfered with American commerce on the high seas in apparent violation of international law. In addition, Americans had special grievances against the British, the oldest of which was impressment.

Chronically short of men, the Royal Navy had long practiced a crude form of military conscription by sending "press gangs" through the streets of British seaports, kidnapping sailors, and the practice even extended to merchant vessels on the high seas. Because of wretched pay and low morale, a sizable portion of the crew went over the side whenever a British man-o'-war put into a foreign port, and many of these deserters wound up in the American merchant service where pay and working conditions were better. Indeed, it has been estimated that between one-half and one-third of America's merchant fleet was manned by foreign, mostly British, seamen. Without the deserters America's trade would have been crippled. The quarrel over impressment involved economics as well as national honor.

To recover these men British captains adopted the practice of stopping American vessels on the sea, mustering the crew, and seizing suspected Englishmen. Though a slap at American sovereignty, the recovery of deserters alone might have been tolerable, but careless British officers dragged many native-born, as well as naturalized, Americans into the Royal Navy (a common newspaper estimate was six thousand by 1806). Not only did this practice endanger the lives of Americans, but it humiliated the government, which found itself helpless to protect its own citizens on the high seas.

Another sore point in Anglo-American relations were the orders-in-council, which sought to employ British naval power to starve the French by blockade. This practice too dated from the beginning of the war, but it was vastly extended when Napoleon gained control of Spain, the Netherlands, and northern Germany. By an order-in-council of 1806, the British blockade was expanded to include the entire northwest coast of Europe, from Denmark to Brittany, though it was actually enforced in the zone between the Seine River and Ostend. International law permitted blockades in time of war, provided each blockaded port was actually invested by warships. With respect to American traffic, British captains found it more rewarding to hover off American ports, stopping outgoing vessels and inspecting their papers to determine whether they were destined for blockaded ports. Then they seized all "contraband" and sometimes the vessel itself. Secretary of State Madison denounced this practice as a "paper blockade" which violated the strictures of international law. The practice of search and seizure of American cargoes on the high seas was as much an affront to American sensitivities as the practice of impressment.

The British stranglehold on the Atlantic sea lanes, moreover, induced Napoleon to retaliate. In Napoleon's mind, Britain had to trade or die, and because much of Britain's trade was with the continent of Europe, he sought to cut Britain off in hopes of crushing its economy. His Berlin Decree of 1806 imposed a French blockade on Britain, to be enforced by seizing any neutral ship that stopped in England before coming to a continental port. The British countered that with an order-in-council of November 1807, which required all neutral vessels destined for a continental port to stop in England first. Napoleon promptly responded with a Milan Decree, which ordered the seizure of any neutral vessel which even submitted to a British search on the high seas. Thus no matter what American captains did they were liable to seizure. Even so, Americans saw a difference between Napoleon's confiscations, which occurred in French ports, and British seizures on the high seas, which were a flagrant violation of American rights.

Even less justified than the orders-in-council, and more selfish, was Britain's desire to retain a monopoly of the world's carrying trade. In the course of the eighteenth century the British merchant fleet, aided by periodic wartime blockades of French and Spanish ports, had become the world's carrier. In the Napoleonic wars British merchants were dismayed to find American ship captains threatening this monopoly by offering cheaper rates and better service. It was with the dual purpose of depriving France of West Indian products and regaining the imperial trade for itself that Britain invoked the Rule of 1756, which prohibited American ships from carrying the products of the French and Spanish islands to Europe. Americans circumvented this regulation by bringing French and Spanish goods to an American port and paying customs duties before reexporting them to the Continent. Ironically, it was mostly Republican merchants, such as the Crowninshields of Salem, who pioneered this trade. Federalists generally adhered to the traditional transatlantic trade with Britain, a trade with which the British did not interfere. Thus, the preservation of America's neutral rights became a partisan issue when Britain turned its attention to the indirect trade.

The reexport trade was held legal by a British prize court in 1800, but the court reversed itself five years later in a decision involving the American ship *Essex*. The *Essex* had left Spain with a cargo destined for Cuba, and it had stopped and paid nominal duties in the United States before it was halted by a British warship. The prize court declared it to be in violation of the Rule of 1756 and ordered it condemned. With orders to enforce the *Essex* decision in the fall of 1805, the Royal Navy seized over two hundred American vessels found carrying French cargoes in the West Indies. This action precipitated the chain of events that eventually led to war.

Eschewing for the moment any thought of war on grounds that the nation was unprepared, Jefferson and Madison decided to revive negotiations in London. To highlight their concern, they sent a special emissary, Maryland lawyer William Pinkney, to join Monroe. Madison instructed Pinkney to secure an agreement on impressment and a modification of the *Essex* decision that would permit Americans to engage in the West Indian trade.

While Pinkney was at sea, Congress decided to give him some bargaining leverage in the form of commercial retaliation. Though the administration seemed indifferent on the subject, various proposals were introduced and debated in the spring of 1806. After John Randolph's defection, there was no effective leader in the House, and without administration guidance Congress floundered in a morass of factional bickering. Jefferson and Madison had no interest in a weak measure of coercion, and Congress had no stomach for a strong one. What finally emerged actually looked more like a bill to foster American manufactures. The Nonimportation Act of 1806 prohibited the import of a select list of British manufactured goods beginning on November 15, unless Britain came to terms in the meantime. Randolph, who had denounced the administration for catering to the interests of northern merchants, scornfully called it "A milk and water bill, a dose of chicken broth to be taken nine months hence."

It is doubtful that any form of coercion would have intimidated Britain at this juncture, but Monroe and Pinkney could well have used a weapon of some kind. They found the British still basking in the afterglow of Trafalgar and unwilling to budge. Their one hope was Charles James Fox, a pro-American Whig, who became prime minister on the death of William Pitt the Younger in January 1806. But that glimmer vanished when Fox died in September. He was succeeded by a coalition misnamed "the ministry of all talents," which had neither the wit to be accommodating nor the strength in Parliament to offer concessions. As a result, Monroe and Pinkney had to ignore their instructions in order to secure any agreement at all. The treaty they signed in December 1806 made no mention of impressment; it did, however, permit the re-export trade in West Indian cargoes provided the goods paid a two percent customs duty in American ports before being shipped to Europe. In return, the United States would agree not to discriminate against British commerce for ten years.

Jefferson and Madison were dismayed with the result. In return for a niggling concession on the West Indian trade they had to surrender their trump card, the threat of commercial retaliation, for a decade. And the treaty ignored the most humiliating circumstances of all—the harassment of American commerce and the kidnapping of American seamen within sight of our own shores. It was not the fault of Monroe and Pinkney; they simply had nothing to offer that Britain wanted. Jefferson still felt that an agreement of this sort was worse than none at all. He did not even submit it to the Senate for ratification.

WHILE MONROE AND PINKNEY WERE struggling for some accommodation with the intractable British, Jefferson was coping with the most severe domestic crisis of his presidency, the conspiracy of Aaron Burr. With his career in ruins following the duel with

Hamilton, Burr turned his attention on the American Southwest where, for more than two decades, conspiracies to secede from the Union alternated with plots to attack Spanish territory in Florida and Texas. The centerpiece of these conspiracies was James Wilkinson, sometime merchant of Louisville, Kentucky, and, as a result of the Indian wars in the Ohio Valley, a general in the army.

Despite western rumors that Wilkinson was in the employ of Spanish authorities in New Orleans (they did, in fact, pay him an annual stipend for information), Wilkinson was the commanding general in the West when Jefferson took office. Jefferson not only retained him in his post but made him governor of the district of Louisiana (the part of the purchase north of the present state of Louisiana, which was then known as the Territory of Orleans). This occasioned some criticism in Congress, not from any hostility to Wilkinson, but because it united civilian and military authority in one person. Jefferson, however, considered the trans-Mississippi West as an Indian preserve for the foreseeable future; thus its governance was purely a military matter. Wilkinson set up his headquarters in St. Louis.

The primary requisites for a successful conspiracy were foreign aid and military opportunity. Neither materialized. Even before leaving office in March 1805 Burr visited the British ambassador, Anthony Merry, to request money and warships. Merry, who detested Americans in general and Jefferson in particular, expressed interest in the scheme, but he naturally needed time to consult London before he committed the British government to an intrigue to divide the United States. Communication with London would take months. In the meantime Burr departed on a tour of the West, visiting prominent figures in Ohio, Kentucky, and Tennessee (including Henry Clay and Andrew Jackson), who naturally welcomed a former vice president. Burr artfully conveyed the idea that he was planning an expedition against Spanish Mexico with the covert support of the government. He met with Wilkinson in St. Louis and journeyed on to New Orleans where he conferred with leaders of the Creole faction, who were unhappy with American rule. Concluding that

New Orleans was ripe for revolution, he returned upriver for another meeting with Wilkinson.

Back in Washington in the fall of 1805, Burr received the disappointing news that the British government, while interested in his plans, was too preoccupied with France to provide aid. Simultaneously, Jefferson's decision to negotiate a purchase of West Florida cooled the crisis with Spain and deprived Burr of an excuse for a military expedition in the Southwest. Undaunted, Burr departed for a second tour of the West in the summer of 1806. From Pittsburgh in July, he sent a coded letter to Wilkinson which informed the general untruthfully that British naval support was on its way to New Orleans, and he himself was proceeding downriver with men and supplies.

Burr's principal agent was an Irish immigrant named Herman Blennerhassett, who owned an island in the Ohio River opposite Marietta. Blennerhassett, with whom Burr visited on each of his western trips, was induced to collect men and supplies for a downriver expedition. What Blennerhassett told his recruits is not clear, but by the summer of 1806 the West was bubbling with rumors of a conspiracy. As early as February Joseph H. Daviess, the federal district attorney in Kentucky, had written Jefferson to warn that Burr and others were plotting to sever the West from the Union. Jefferson showed the letter to his cabinet and asked Daviess for more information. All he received was more rumor and speculation, none of it usable in a court of law. Jefferson received reports from other sources throughout the summer, but still he hesitated to act. Jefferson worried that if he moved prematurely, before the conspirators had committed an overt act, the conspirators could deny everything and go free. He also had faith in the people of the West, feeling that the vast majority of them would not tolerate, much less join, a conspiracy to sever the Union.

In October Postmaster General Gideon Granger provided Jefferson with a transcription of a conversation Burr had had with a military adventurer who was disgruntled with the government. Burr had discussed the possible overthrow of the government in Washington. Jefferson could delay no longer. The pieces were beginning to fit. Burr was at the center of a conspiracy of some sort, although the exact object was not yet clear. After clearing the idea with the cabinet, Jefferson dispatched the secretary of the Orleans Territory, John Graham, to shadow Burr. After weeks of gathering information, Graham awakened the governor of Ohio to the preparations on Blennerhassett's island, and, in early December, the governor sent the state militia to raid the place. Blennerhassett escaped down the Ohio River with only one boatload of men. Burr was then recruiting in Kentucky and planned to rendezvous with Blennerhassett at the mouth of the Cumberland River. Burr had acquired title to a Spanish land grant in Texas, and he apparently was telling his recruits that they were going to settle these newly opened lands. Burr in fact maintained, to the end of his life, that this was the only purpose of the expedition.

General Wilkinson received Burr's July letter in September while he was on the Texas frontier carrying out the President's orders for a military demonstration against the Spanish. (The order had been issued months earlier as part of Jefferson's West Florida strategy.) Wilkinson worked out a truce with the Spanish commander, and then covered his tracks by writing directly to the President. Wilkinson, after all, had little to gain from Burr's conspiracy and much to lose; by betraying Burr he could portray himself as savior of the Union and simultaneously make a claim to his Spanish paymasters that he had thwarted an attack on Mexico. (He in fact sent authorities in Mexico City a bill for $120,000 for his services.)

His letter to Jefferson, written on October 21, warned the President of an impending attack on Mexico, and he enclosed Burr's coded letter of July, carefully edited to omit all passages that incriminated himself. He then sped to New Orleans where he declared martial law and arrested all the prominent leaders of the Creole element. Two of Burr's closest confederates, Erich Bollman and Samuel Swartwout, were shipped east to stand trial. All fronts secured, Wilkinson sat back to wait for the unsuspecting Burr to float downriver into his clutches.

Jefferson received Wilkinson's letter on November 25. This

was the first official word of a conspiracy from the military commander on the spot; he realized it was time to act. He issued a proclamation directing federal and state officials to arrest anyone conspiring to attack Spanish territory. Wilkinson had not specifically mentioned Burr nor talked of treason, so neither did the President. Anxious weeks of waiting ensued. Jefferson mentioned the conspiracy in his annual message to Congress, and when Congress asked for more information he supplied all that he had. Concerned that the administration had not moved forcefully enough, the Senate approved a bill suspending the writ of *habeas corpus*, a move that would have allowed government marshalls to arrest anyone suspected of treason without having to show cause. When William A. Burwell, a Virginian who had assumed the role of administration spokesman in the House, showed the measure to the President, Jefferson told him it was unnecessary and passage would give him great pain. Burwell, joined by the President's son-in-law, John Wayles Eppes, persuaded the House to vote it down.

Burr's party stopped in Natchez, Mississippi Territory, in early January. Handed a newspaper containing Jefferson's proclamation of November 27, Burr realized that he had been betrayed. He surrendered to Mississippi authorities, was released because he had done nothing illegal there, and started overland toward Florida. Near Mobile, Alabama, he was recognized by an army lieutenant, arrested, and shipped back east for trial. "On the whole," wrote Jefferson echoing a passage from his First Inaugural, "this squall, by showing with what ease our government suppresses movements which in other countries require armies, has greatly increased its strength by increasing the public confidence in it." The result vindicated the Jeffersonian notion that a free republic could govern a vast territory simply by winning the confidence of the people. The danger had passed, but whether Burr could be punished was another matter. To Jefferson, accumulating evidence that would stand up in a court of law had been the central problem from the very beginning.

Burr was tried before the federal circuit court meeting in Richmond, Virginia, Chief Justice John Marshall presiding. The southern circuit had jurisdiction of the case because the locus of the conspiracy, Blennerhassett's island, was in Virginia. A grand jury, headed by Jefferson's foremost critic, John Randolph, assembled in May 1807 to hear testimony from the government's star witness, James Wilkinson. Under examination from Burr's shrewd defense counsel, the general was forced to admit that he had deleted parts of Burr's letter before sending it to the President and that the code between him and Burr was devised as early as 1794. The grand jury came within a few votes of indicting the government witness himself, and then voted to indict Burr and Blennerhassett for treason.

With Marshall and Randolph orchestrating the show, Jefferson felt that the administration was on trial with Burr. He accordingly took an active role in the prosecution, setting up a dispatch rider between Washington and Richmond so he could be in daily contact with federal attorney George Hay. When the trial opened on August 3, Jefferson and Hay relied heavily on the testimony of Erich Bollman, the confederate of Burr's whom Wilkinson had arrested in New Orleans. Jefferson had interviewed Bollman personally and got the full story of the conspiracy. He offered Bollman a pardon if he would tell his story in court. In Richmond, however, Bollman rejected the pardon and declined to testify, citing his Fifth Amendment protection against self-incrimination. As it turned out, much of the evidence assembled by the prosecution was irrelevant anyway because of John Marshall's ruling on the law of the case.

The crime of treason as defined by the Constitution requires two witnesses to the same "overt act." The intention of the Framers was clearly to make conviction for treason difficult, for the crime had been a political weapon throughout much of English history, wielded by those in power against their enemies. After hearing testimony for nearly a month, John Marshall read his legal opinion on August 31. Interpreting the Constitution as narrowly as possible, Marshall ruled that the mere assemblage of men or the inoperative intention to divide the Union did not constitute an "overt act" of treason. Moreover, since Burr was not present on Blennerhassett's island during the preparations for the expedition, no two of the government's witnesses could testify to seeing him at the same moment, and Marshall held that he could not be there by "constructive presence." Since this ruling disposed of much of the testimony for the prosecution, the government dropped the case.

Marshall did remand Burr and Blennerhassett for trial in Ohio on a charge of misdemeanor. Burr posted bail, forfeited it, and fled to England. He returned in 1812 after friends in New York persuaded the state to drop the criminal charges that had been hanging over him since the Hamilton duel. He lived another twenty-four years in utter obscurity. If Jefferson found any pleasure in the mantle of disgrace that Burr carried to his grave, he never mentioned it. He took comfort instead in the larger good wrought by the Burr Conspiracy, the proof of the loyalty of Americans to their republic.

IN THE SAME WEEK THAT BURR WAS INDICTED for treason in Richmond, foreign affairs reclaimed Jefferson's attention. Earlier that year, because of deteriorating relations with Britain, the administration had decided to bring back into service some of the warships built by the Federalists, among them the *Chesapeake*, a 38-gun frigate. The vessel was being fitted out in Norfolk, and its officers accidentally signed on four men who had deserted from a British warship, the *Leopard*, which was in port taking on water and victuals. Three of the deserters were in fact Americans who had been pressed into British service. Vice Admiral George Berkeley, commander of the fleet in American waters and a typical specimen of British arrogance, personally ordered what could only be described as an act of war. When the *Chesapeake* departed on a "shakedown" cruise on June 22, the *Leopard* followed her out of the harbor. At sea the *Leopard* came up to the American vessel and demanded a search. When the American captain, who had not even opened his gunports, refused, the *Leopard* poured broadside after broadside into the American ship for ten minutes, killing three and wounding twenty more before the *Chesapeake* could strike its flag. Officers of the *Leopard* then boarded the American warship, arrested the four deserters, and sailed off into the blue, leaving the *Chesapeake* to limp back into Norfolk. In Halifax the British deserter was hanged; the Americans were condemned and pardoned on condition of returning to British service.

News of the outrage sent a shock wave of indignation the length of the continent. War seemed inevitable even to those who had sought peace at any price. Jefferson issued a proclamation banning British warships from American waters and summoned Congress into session a month earlier than usual. The cabinet dispatched the frigate *Revenge* to Britain with instructions to Monroe to demand a disavowal of the attack, return of the four seamen, Berkeley's recall, and promises that such outrages would not occur in the future. Jefferson then repaired to his mountaintop for the "sickly" months of August and September. Reflecting on the nation's plight in the isolation of Monticello, Jefferson concluded that Britain was unlikely to yield to American demands and that war was unavoidable. That prospect did not dismay him; he could even see some advantages for the United States. Since Spain was militarily helpless, war would give the United States an excuse to seize the Floridas, long coveted by Jefferson. "I had rather have war against Spain than not, if we go to war against England," he told Madison. "Our southern defensive force can take the Floridas, volunteers for a Mexican army will flock to our standard, and a rich pabulum will be offered to our privateers in the plunder of their commerce and coasts. Probably Cuba would add itself to our confederation." By the end of the summer, however, he was leaning toward economic coercion; war would be a last resort.

The war fever in the country had cooled noticeably by the time Congress convened on October 26, and Congress was clearly disposed toward peace, or, at most, commercial retaliation. Jefferson's annual message, crafted with considerable help from the cabinet, was a delicate balance between patriotic indignation and hopes for peace. Nothing could be done until word was received from Britain; both President and Congress marked time for nearly six weeks. Toward the end of November word informally trickled in that the British would not apologize for the attack on the *Chesapeake* and would not reprimand the commanders on the American station. Indeed, the British ministry was contemplating an even more stringent order-in-council regulating American trade. Jefferson's cabinet met for three successive days in mid-December to consider the options of war or embargo, and it finally decided on the latter. Commercial retaliation had a long and honorable history, dating to pre-Revolutionary days, and it had been Republican dogma since the Jay Treaty crisis of 1794. The only member of the cabinet who had misgivings was Gallatin, who thought war preferable to a permanent embargo. However, Jefferson was unwilling to affix a termination date, lest that weaken the embargo's coercive effect.

On December 18 Jefferson sent a confidential message to Congress recommending an embargo for the protection of American shipping and seamen who were threatened on the high seas. If this was to be a prelude to war, Jefferson did not say so; nor did he mention coercing Britain and France into a recognition of American rights. Nevertheless, an embargo had been extensively discussed throughout the fall, and both houses of Congress seemed to know what was wanted. Behind closed doors, the Senate approved the Embargo Act on the same day by 22 to 6, and the House acted three days later, 82 to 44 (Federalists and Randolph in opposition). The law enacted a self-imposed blockade on American commerce, prohibiting American vessels from sailing to foreign ports and preventing foreign vessels from taking on cargoes in the United States.

Thus, with relatively little discussion and no public explanation, Jefferson led the country into an experiment with enormous consequences for the nation's economy and foreign policy. Neither Jefferson nor Congress anticipated the hardship the embargo would bring to the country. Federalist tales of goods rotting on wharves and ships leaking from disuse were exaggerated, but there is no doubt that the economy was seriously damaged. Because the country lacked a network of roads, most interstate trade had to go by water. The government even halted this coastal trade for fear that an enterprising captain might run his coastal schooner to Europe or the West Indies. In New England and Pennsylvania mercantile capital was diverted to manufactures; textile mills and iron foundries increased rapidly. Local manufactures sprang up everywhere, but despite the growth of economic independence, the South suffered severely. Its exports were perishable, and its slaves had to be fed and clothed even when masters could not sell their produce. Jefferson's own fortune never fully recovered from the disastrous impact of the embargo.

Jefferson's real failure was one of communication. He never adequately explained to Congress or the public what he expected to accomplish with the embargo. If he had ever regarded it as a prelude to war, he had totally abandoned that objective by mid-1808. His correspondence indicates that he regarded it as a weapon of peaceable coercion, an effort to win recognition of American rights by halting the flow of American goods to both European belligerents. But, other than impressment, what rights? He might have used the British order-in-council of November 11, 1807, as justification for the imposition of the embargo. This order required all neutral vessels bound for Continental ports to pass through British ports, pay taxes, and secure a clearance. Without such a license, neutral vessels were fair prize for British warships. By subjecting American trade to colonial regulation, the order was a savage blow to American independence. Retaliation, perhaps even war, was justified. American newspapers published this British directive on December 17, the day before Jefferson sent his embargo message to Congress. Jefferson, unfortunately, never officially communicated the order to Congress, nor did he cite it publicly as a justification for the embargo.

"I did not expect a crop of so sudden and rank growth of fraud and open opposition by force could have grown up in the United States," Jefferson wrote Gallatin in the late summer of 1808. Faced with growing criticism and widespread evasion of the law, the administration tightened its grip. The Enforcement Act of 1808 gave customs officials extensive powers of search and seizure in enforcing the law. Indeed, such arbitrary powers may well have infringed on the Fourth Amendment's protection against unreasonable searches and seizures, but the issue was never tested in the courts. Ironically, the possibility of a constitutional problem never occurred to Jefferson or Madison. With equal vigor, Gallatin, who was in charge of enforcement, ordered the army into action to suppress a flourishing overland trade between New England and Canada.

As an experiment in pacifism, the embargo certainly had grand potential, and it might have worked had it lasted long enough. Within a year there were food riots in northern England, and textile mills in Lancashire stood idle for lack of raw cotton. British business interests might have begun to put pressure on the government but for an accident of history that Jefferson could not have foreseen. Napoleon's attempt to install his brother on the throne of Spain offended Spanish pride and triggered an uprising against French authority (the word "guerrilla" or "mini-war" was coined to describe it). Britain went to the aid of the rebels and eventually landed an army, commanded by the Duke of Wellington, on the Iberian peninsula. As Spain fell into Britain's orbit, British business interests saw a vast new market being opened, in Spain and Latin America, that more than compensated for the loss of the United States. That gave the British ministry time to endure whatever hardships the embargo caused, time that Jefferson did not have because his people were suffering more than the British.

Throughout Jefferson's second term, it was common knowledge in the nation's capital that he intended to follow the precedent set by Washington and retire after eight years. The determination was certainly an honorable one. "If anything were wanting to stamp Jefferson great and good," wrote one admirer; "to place him highest on the list of benefactors of mankind, the voluntary surrender of the first office in the gift of a free people, entitles him to precedence." The hearsay diminished Jefferson's influence and probably contributed to the party schisms that marred his second term. Jefferson might have enhanced his leverage by being coy about his future, but that was not in his nature. He damaged himself further by announcing in December 1807, prior to his embargo message, that he planned to retire at the end of his term. In January a caucus of congressional Repub-

licans nominated Madison for president and renominated George
Clinton for the second office.

Despite the unpopularity of the embargo and the personal
vilification that Jefferson suffered throughout the year 1808, the
electorate was not disposed to return to Federalism. But the
election did severely test Republican unity. George Clinton refused formally to accept the vice presidential nomination and
toyed with the idea of a presidential candidacy of his own. James
Monroe, angered by Jefferson's cavalier treatment of his 1806
treaty, returned from Britain and allowed the Randolph element
in Virginia to support his candidacy. Monroe picked up some
popular votes in Virginia, but no electoral votes anywhere. Madison handily defeated the Federalist candidate, Charles Cotesworth
Pinckney, by 122 electoral votes to 47.

Jefferson took great comfort in the knowledge that he would
be succeeded by his best friend and ally, but he made the transfer
of power more difficult by his own inaction. Although his behavior was probably dictated by the memory of how John Adams's
actions had compromised and clouded his own inauguration,
Jefferson went too far in the other direction. He virtually abdi-
cated his office after the result of the election became known.
He began by announcing that no federal vacancies would be
filled until the new president was sworn in.

When Congress assembled in December 1808, it was clear
that a choice had to be made between going to war, continuing
the embargo, or meekly submitting to British regulations. Although Jefferson regarded either war or submission as unthink-
able, he decided not to make any recommendation to Congress.
"On this occasion," he wrote, "I think it is fair to leave to those
who are to act on them, the decisions they prefer, meaning to be
myself but a spectator. I should not feel justified in directing
measures which those who are to execute them would disap-
prove." His annual message, as a result, spoke of the failure of
the embargo but offered no remedy. This left Congress in confusion. "The President gives no opinion as to the measures that
ought to be adopted," complained Nathaniel Macon. "It is not
known whether he be for war or peace."

The cabinet, which Jefferson had utilized so effectively in past crises, was rudderless. "Both Mr. Madison and myself concur in the opinion," Gallatin wrote the President, "that, considering the temper of the Legislature, or rather of its members, it would be eligible to point out to them some precise and distinct course." Gallatin confessed that he himself had not decided between the embargo and war, but, he continued, "I think that we must (or rather you must) decide the question absolutely, so that we may point out a decisive course either way to our friends." When Jefferson declined the request, Gallatin and Madison did their best to fill the power vacuum. In January Congress passed an Enforcement Act drafted by Gallatin, which gave customs officials arbitrary powers of search and seizure. It was the last vote the administration would win, however; thereafter the fate of the embargo was in the hands of the faction-ridden hornet's nest on Capitol Hill.

Supporters of the administration did make an effort to extend the embargo for a few more months. On January 20 the House passed a resolution calling for a special session of the new Congress (the current Congress would expire on March 3) to meet on the fourth Monday of May. Wilson Cary Nicholas then offered a resolution that the embargo would be repealed on a date to be determined, and that privateers would be authorized to prey on the commerce of nations that persisted in their decrees. The assumption was, Jefferson wrote to his son-in-law, that the issue of letters of marque to privateers would be a prelude to war. Nicholas then moved to fill the repeal date with June 1. At that point New England Republicans rebelled, joined by New York Clintonians and Federalists. This tenuous majority rejected Nicholas's motion and substituted the fourth of March. The embargo and Jefferson would exit together.

Since abject submission was still out of the question, the administration searched desperately for an alternative. Nonintercourse, which Jefferson had considered and rejected in November, seemed to be the only one. As passed near the end of February, the Non-Intercourse Act severed trade with Britain and France only, and it authorized the President to open trade with either belligerent upon repeal of the cabinet's orders-in-council or Napoleon's decrees.

The agony of the embargo and its ignominious demise, cast a pall over Jefferson's last months in office and made him more eager than ever to return to Monticello. On his next to last full day in office, he wrote: "Within a few days I retire to my family, my books and farms. . . . Never did a prisoner, released from his chains, feel such relief as I shall on shaking off the shackles of power." Madison asked him to ride with him in his carriage to the inauguration, but Jefferson declined, saying that all the honors of the day belonged to him. Jefferson instead rode down Pennsylvania Avenue on horseback, accompanied only by his grandson, Thomas Jefferson Randolph. Sitting on the dais next to Madison in the newly completed hall of the House of Representatives, Jefferson seemed to one observer to be "one of the most happy among this concourse of people."

After the inauguration Jefferson was among the large number of well-wishers who called on the Madisons at their house, and that evening he attended the inaugural ball. He took a week to wind up his personal affairs and complete his packing. He then set out for Monticello followed by a caravan of wagons. Writing to an old friend, he summed up his forty-year political career: "Nature intended me for the tranquil pursuits of science, by rendering them my supreme delight. But the enormities of the times in which I have lived have forced me to take a part in resisting them, and to commit myself on the boisterous ocean of political passions." No year had been more turbulent than his last, but now that too was over.

Chapter Eight

---○---

Twilight

"I REMEMBER WELL," ONE OF JEFFERSON'S granddaughters later recalled, "when he first returned to Monticello, how immediately he began to prepare new beds for his flowers." Tending his gardens and his grandchildren, that was how Jefferson planned to spend his twilight years. Both demanded—and received—a great deal of attention. He had planned the flower gardens on the spacious west lawn in 1807, but did not complete them until five years later. He laid them out in ovals, on either side of a winding walk. He also put in a vegetable garden on the sunny southern slope of the mountain, and he replanted the orchard that had suffered from age and neglect during his years of public service.

Of grandchildren there was an abundance. Martha and Thomas Mann Randolph had built a plantation at Edgehill, a few miles from Monticello on the banks of the Rivanna River. Martha contrived to be at Monticello when her father was home for visits, and when he retired in March 1809 she moved into her father's house with her eight children. She resided in Monticello and managed the household until Jefferson's death. Randolph, a moody man who apparently resented the closeness of Martha and her father, divided his time between farming and politics, serving several terms in Congress and ultimately as governor of Virginia (1819–1822). The Randolphs ultimately had eleven children, and with Francis Eppes, Mary's offspring, a part-time resident, Jefferson's grandchildren totaled an even dozen. Jefferson became a great-grandfather in 1812. Eight years later he told Maria Cosway, who had resumed their long-lapsed correspondence, that he had "about half a dozen" great grandchildren and that he lived "like a patriarch of old" among his youthful descendants.

His grandchildren adored Jefferson. "Cheerfulness, love, benevolence, wisdom, seemed to animate his whole form," one of them recalled. "I cannot describe the feelings of veneration, admiration, and love that existed in my heart towards him. I looked upon him as being too great and too good for my comprehension; and yet I felt no fear to approach him, and be taught by him some of the childish sports I delighted in." When Jefferson went walking in the garden, he called to the children to follow him. He helped them pick fruit in the orchard and organized footraces on the lawn, carefully staggering the distances according to age so each had a chance to win. He rewarded the winners with three of the best fruits he had picked. Losers got one.

In 1810, after a year's retirement, Jefferson described his daily routine to Thaddeus Kosciusko, the Polish volunteer who had served nobly in the Revolution. "My mornings are devoted to correspondence. From breakfast to dinner, I am in my shops, my garden, or on horseback among my farms; from dinner to dark, I give to society and recreation with my neighbors and friends; and from candle light to early bed-time, I read." Jefferson carried on a voluminous correspondence throughout his later years, though his letters on any given day frequently duplicated one another. Throughout his late years he used a polygraph machine that made an original and a copy simultaneously.

However, one correspondent, John Adams, demanded originality. The viciousness of the election of 1800 and Adams's unsportsmanlike "midnight appointments" seemed to doom any further contact between the two onetime allies. The ice broke momentarily in 1804 when Mary's death caused Abigail Adams, who had taken care of her in London years before, to write Jefferson a letter of condolence. Jefferson responded warmly, indicating "an uniform and high measure of respect and good will" for John Adams even though he still resented Adams's midnight appointments. Abigail replied with some resentments of her own, and the correspondence ended five months later when John Adams discovered the letters. After Jefferson left office, Dr. Benjamin Rush, a signer of the Declaration of Independence and friend to both men, thought it time to repair the relationship. After an initial rebuff from Adams, Rush wrote to Jefferson expressing the hope that the two ex-presidents might renew their friendship through correspondence. Jefferson replied by sending Rush copies of his exchange with Abigail to demonstrate that he had "not been wanting either in the desire, or the endeavor to remove this misunderstanding." Rush forwarded the packet to Adams. Still hesitant, Adams waited until New Years Day, 1812, before writing a brief note wishing Jefferson a happy new year. He also mailed Jefferson two volumes of *Lectures on Rhetoric and Oratory* written by his son, John Quincy Adams, while a professor at Harvard College. Jefferson was delighted, responded warmly, and the two corresponded regularly for the rest of their lives. It was a remarkable exchange, ranging from politics to history, religion, and science. They bombarded each other with ideas, Adams more often than not fanciful and theoretical, Jefferson's tending more to scientific dissertations. But each letter evoked a response that kept them intellectually challenged until the day in 1826 that they both died.

DESPITE THIS IDYLLIC EXISTENCE, Jefferson was not dead to the world about him. Describing his relations with his neighbors, he wrote: "I talk of ploughs and harrows, of seeding and harvesting with my neighbors, and of politics too, if they choose, with as little reserve as the rest of my fellow citizens and feel, at length, the blessings of being free to say and do what I please, without being responsible to any mortal." He was a bit more diffident, however, with his successor in Washington. He had a stake in Madison's success as president, since Madison had fallen heir both to the Jeffersonian fiscal system and the policy of commercial retaliation, but he hesitated to interfere. Since the two thought alike, there was really little need for a correspondence on matters of policy. Madison and his wife Dolley stopped at Monticello each summer for a visit, and these no doubt afforded an opportunity to renew the long-standing collaboration.

Jefferson's most important service to his successor was to mend relations between Madison and Monroe. The latter had been deeply offended by the rejection of his 1806 treaty, which John Randolph attributed to Madison's intercession. Randolph, John Taylor, and other "Old Republicans" persuaded Monroe that Madison had compromised the party's principles and was following a path to Federalism. After the election of 1808 revealed the weakness of the "Old Republicans," even in Virginia (most of Monroe's votes came from Federalist counties west of the Blue Ridge), Jefferson made it his business to draw Monroe away from the Randolph clique. Monroe rebuffed the initial efforts, but his ego was salved when Republicans rallied behind him and elected him governor in 1810. When Madison offered him the State Department, Monroe could resist no longer.

The State Department had been a headache to Madison from the inception of his presidency. The initial understanding was that Gallatin would get the job. However, navy secretary Robert Smith also coveted the post, and Smith had the support of a faction in the Senate headed by his brother. Madison relented and named Smith to the State Department, leaving Gallatin at the Treasury. Smith, however, proved to be utterly inept, and Madison found himself drafting most of the administration's foreign policy papers. The Smith faction, whom Nathaniel Macon dubbed "the invisibles," remained comparatively loyal for a year, but in 1810 they began sniping at Gallatin from the floor of the Senate. Finding his position intolerable, Gallatin in the spring of 1811 threatened to resign. Forced with having to choose between his two cabinet members, Madison dismissed Smith and offered the State Department to Monroe. Monroe accepted and resigned the governorship. Since the State Department had become recognized as a step toward the presidency, Monroe's eventual accession to the office was apparent. The Republican triumvirate would become a dynasty; Jefferson was delighted.

Jefferson followed closely Madison's tortuous path through various forms of commercial retaliation until he eventually became convinced that the nation had no choice but to go to war. He greeted the outbreak of war in 1812 with mixed feelings. On the one hand, it stirred his ever-present nationalism. War, he thought, would shatter British influence in America:

> the second weaning from British principles, British attachments, British manners and manufactures will be salutary, and will form an epoch of the spirit of nationalism and of consequent prosperity, which would never have resulted from a continued subordination to the interests and influence of England.

He also saw war as a chance to expand American territory at the expense of the British. "The acquisition of Canada this year, so far as the neighborhood of Quebec, will be a mere matter of marching," he boasted. Halifax, Nova Scotia, would fall in the next campaign, and then the United States could turn its attention to Florida.

He viewed the war as not one against Britain alone, but in a larger sense against Europe, a war to free the New World from European regulation and tyranny. It would be expensive, he realized, and the cost tempered his nationalism. "Farewell all hope of extinguishing the public debt!" he moaned. "Farewell all visions of applying the surplus revenue to the improvements of peace, rather than the ravages of war. Our enemy has indeed the consolation of Satan on removing our first parents from Paradise; from a peaceful and agricultural nation he makes us a military and manufacturing one."

Military disasters soon dashed these grandiose dreams, and economic hardship brought a dose of chill reality. The Bank of the United States had gone out of business when its charter expired in 1811, to Jefferson's satisfaction, but in its absence state banks proliferated. They flooded the country with generally worthless paper, and Congress added to the inflation by financing the war with paper money. Inflation added to Jefferson's expenses, and his income failed to keep up because of the British blockade, which barred access to foreign markets. Jefferson pleaded with Madison to use the navy to break the British blockade, but the administration found that the few ships it had were better employed engaging isolated British vessels on the high seas. By 1814 Jefferson and his neighbors were feeding their wheat to their horses. Converting it to whiskey was one alternative, but the surplus was such, quipped Jefferson, that "all mankind must become drunkards to consume it." The war was, for him, a personal disaster that greatly increased his indebtedness.

THE SPECTER OF DEBT SHADOWED Jefferson all his life, and it became more threatening every year as he grew older. When he wound up his affairs in Washington, he discovered that he had a multitude of overlooked debts, forcing him to borrow an additional $10,000. Some he got from a private lender in Virginia, the rest from the Bank of the United States, on a note countersigned by Madison. His total indebtedness now exceeded $25,000, and his Bedford County plantation, Poplar Forest, was mortgaged to his creditors. Recalling in later years the shock of discovering his indebtedness upon leaving the presidency, Jefferson ascribed it to his having turned the President's house into "a general tavern" for the Washington community. Unfortunately, he made no effort to curb his hospitality in retirement. Monticello was a Mecca for every traveler in America, and Virginia friends descended upon him by the wagonload. Often his stable, which could accommodate twenty-six horses in addition to his own, was full. Martha put up as many as fifty guests a night somewhere on the mountaintop. Jefferson's farm manager, Edmund Bacon, thought the expenses of entertaining were the biggest single factor in Jefferson's descent into poverty.

Jefferson had long experimented with various manufactures to supplement his income. His naillery was still operating when he retired, but it was only sporadically successful. The British blockade in the Chesapeake cut off his supply of iron from Philadelphia during the war, and he was forced to close down until 1815. The shop operated intermittently thereafter until

1823. It rarely turned a profit because Jefferson's customers were as shy of cash as he.

Jefferson's other manufacturing enterprises were developed more to fill his own needs than to augment his income. In 1803 he rebuilt for his own use a gristmill originally established by his father. Three years later he invested $10,000 in a large manufacturing mill with the latest equipment, some of it invented by the Maryland flour mill entrepreneur, Oliver Evans. When Evans sued on his patent, Jefferson replied with a treatise on the law of patents. He pointed out that his mill had been erected after Evans's patent expired. After consulting books on mechanical arts, Jefferson informed Evans's attorney that the principles of Evans's patent were very old and had been put to many uses around the world. A person cannot maintain a monopoly or a patent on an idea, Jefferson lectured the attorney. Even so, maintenance of the equipment, mismanagement by persons to whom Jefferson leased the mill, and patent litigation ate up most of the profits.

Jefferson had long wished to produce textiles and clothing for his slave "family" at Monticello, but he did not undertake it on a large scale until the War of 1812. By the end of the war he and Randolph together had four spinning jennies in operation, with a total of 112 spindles, and sufficient looms to weave 2,000 yards of cottons, linens, and woolens yearly. A descendent of the Hemings family remembered many years later that Jefferson in the years of his retirement had "but little taste or care for agricultural pursuits. . . . It was mechanics he seemed to direct, and in their operations he took great interest." In 1815 he turned the management of his farms over to his twenty-three-year-old grandson, Thomas Jefferson Randolph, and virtually gave up agriculture altogether.

In managing his numerous factories Jefferson applied the free market philosophy that he and other Republicans had been developing since the 1790s. Since wealth was derived from "the natural wants" of men, he reasoned that the productivity of a worker was directly proportionate to the financial incentive. The principle applied even when the labor force was enslaved.

Even the South was beginning to see the water-powered mills and smoky tenement houses that signaled industrialization, a change in the landscape that Jefferson dreaded. *Union Manufactories of Maryland on Patapsco Falls, Baltimore County*, pencil sketch by Maxamilliam Godofroy. *Courtesy of the Maryland Historical Society, Baltimore.*

Jefferson accordingly devised a variety of incentives for his artisans. One descendant remembered that Jefferson "gave the boys in the nail factory a pound of meat a week, a dozen herrings, a quart of molasses, and a peck of meal. Give them that wukked the best a suit of red or blue; encouraged them mightily." The clothing prize probably had special appeal because slaves were normally given a new set of clothing only twice a year.

Each of the adult artisans received an incentive. The blacksmith Little George, manager of the naillery, received a percentage of its profits. The coopers were allowed to sell every thirty-third flour barrel they manufactured. Most imaginative of all was Jefferson's treatment of his charcoal makers. Rewarding them for efficiency as well as productivity, he paid them according to the average number of bushels of charcoal they could extract from a cord of wood. John Hemings, the joiner, and Burwell Colbert, butler and painter, each received a monthly wage of between fifteen and twenty dollars as well as an annual "gratuity" of the same amount. There is no record of how effective these incentives were, but a number of observers reported that the artisan slaves at Monticello worked with relatively little supervision. That in itself was cost-saving.

During the war Jefferson took pride in the spread of household manufactures nationwide in response to the British blockade. He once remarked that spinners and weavers did more damage to the British than all the generals put together. He also delighted in the shift of capital in the eastern states from commerce to manufacturing during the war. He supported the tariff of 1816, guided through Congress by Republican nationalist Henry Clay to protect the country's infant manufacturers from foreign competition. Modifying what he had written about the supremacy of agriculture in the *Notes on Virginia,* Jefferson claimed that in the thirty-year interim America had discovered that other countries had

> both profligacy and power enough to exclude us from the field of interchange with other nations: that to be independent for the comforts of life we must fabricate them ourselves. We must place the manufacturer by the side of the agriculturalist. . . . Experience has taught me that manufactures are now as necessary to our independence as to our comfort.

A desire for commercial independence drove his new interest in manufactures, but he had not abandoned his ideal of an agrarian republic. The sort of manufactures he had in mind were household. His vision of the future did not include smoke-belching factories and sprawling cities. "I view great cities," he once wrote Benjamin Rush, "as pestilential to the morals, the health, and the liberties of man."

IN HIS FRANTIC EFFORTS TO RELIEVE HIMSELF from debt Jefferson found that his most saleable asset was his extensive library. He had collected books all his life, and his library contained 6,500 volumes, easily the most extensive collection in the country. It was arranged in three main divisions, History, Philosophy, and Fine Arts, and shelved in his study in pine cases nine feet high. The cases also served as carrying cartons, needing only to be boarded and nailed in front before being shipped.

When the British captured Washington and burned the Capitol building in August 1814, they destroyed the little library that Congress had accumulated. Jefferson wrote to Washington journalist Samuel Harrison Smith offering his own library and asking him to act as his agent. A resolution for the purchase of the library met some opposition in Congress from Federalists, who alleged that it contained numerous philosophical and infidel volumes of no use to Congress and dangerous to the public. The resolution passed nevertheless. Congress retained a Washington bookseller to appraise the library. Using Jefferson's catalogue and arbitrarily assigning a price based on the size of each book, the bookseller evaluated the library at $24,000. Had he evaluated each volume by original cost or replacement value, the appraisal would probably have been double that. Nevertheless, Jefferson did not object. Perhaps he felt it would have been unseemly, since his offer was motivated in part by patriotism. He devoted three-fourths of the proceeds to debt retirement, but he could not forbear spending several hundred dollars for new books. His third library would eventually reach a thousand volumes.

It required ten wagons to haul the books off the mountain, and the departure left a void in Jefferson's life. The absence of his library, however, did not much hinder his intellectual pursuits. Following the War of 1812 he spent the better part of three years on the completion of his religious odyssey. What has become known as "The Jefferson Bible" originated in a promise to Benjamin Rush, an evangelical Christian, in the course of evening conversations in the winter of 1798–1799, which, as Jefferson remembered, served as an antidote to the daily tensions in Congress. Rush believed that a successful republic had to be founded on Christianity. Jefferson could not agree, but he did promise to give Rush a summary of his religious views that would be very different from the "anti-Christian system" ascribed to him by his Federalist opponents.

He took up the task in April 1803 after receiving a copy of Joseph Priestley's latest book, *Socrates and Jesus Compared*. Although in his youth Jefferson had favored the pre-Christian moralists, such as Socrates, he now felt that the ethics of Jesus, if separated from the corruptions and superstitions of the Christian churches, "would be the most perfect and sublime that has ever been taught by man." He ruminated on Priestley's book on the ride from Monticello to Washington, and upon his arrival promptly put his ideas in outline form. He called it a "Syllabus of an Estimate of the Merit of the Doctrines of Jesus, Compared with those of Others," and he sent copies to Rush, Priestley, and several members of his cabinet.

In spare time during the remainder of his presidency he worked on the second part of the work. The premise of the Syllabus was that the teachings of Jesus had been corrupted by theologians and churches; thus it was necessary to find the pure texts. Jefferson took up a New Testament and cut from the four books of the Evangelists those verses that had the authentic stamp of Jesus' thinking, "as easily distinguished," he thought, "as diamonds in a dunghill." He arranged these in a text of forty-six pages that he called the "Philosophy of Jesus."

With encouragement from John Adams, among others, Jefferson returned to the task in 1816. What he wanted was a Bible of primitive Christianity, free of the mysticism of the later Testaments (the Book of Revelations, for instance) and the priestly canons of the third and fourth centuries. The scissors-and-paste job took three years, apparently because of the difficulty of finding Greek and Latin translations. Completed, it went to 164 pages, two columns to the page, and he entitled it "The Life and Morals of Jesus of Nazareth." It was done exclusively for his own benefit; his family did not learn of it until after his death. This work, together with the Syllabus, constituted "The Jefferson Bible."

Whether his embrace of the teachings of Jesus made him a Christian did not concern Jefferson. He once said he was a sect unto himself so far as he knew. He contributed to various denominations in his neighborhood, as he had in his youth, and

occasionally attended their services. He followed the birth of
Unitarianism in New England with great interest and applauded
when both John Adams and his son joined the Unitarian congregation in Quincy. But in the end reason was his church; it was
God's only gift to man. As he wrote in 1814:

> I have followed it faithfully in all important cases, to such a
> degree at least as leaves me without uneasiness, and if on
> minor occasions I have erred from its dictates, I have trust in
> him who made us what we are, and know it was not his plan to
> make us always unerring. He has formed us moral agents . . .
> [so] that we may promote the happiness of those with whom
> he has placed us in society, by acting honestly towards all,
> benevolently to those who fall within our way, respecting
> sacredly their rights bodily and mental, and cherishing espe-
> cially their freedom of conscience, as we value our own.

IT WOULD HAVE IMPOSED A NICE SYMMETRY on his life if Jefferson
had picked up in his twilight years the unfinished agenda for
liberal reform set forth in the Revolutionary years. The state
constitution of 1776 was still in place and still badly in need of
reform. Jefferson's strictures of 1776 were still valid. The Virginia
executive was too weak, and the legislature was in the control of
conservative Tidewater planters. By 1816 much of the population
and most of the wealth of the state lay in the fertile valley
counties west of the Blue Ridge. Calls for reform were being
heard from west of the Blue Ridge, but Jefferson had no inclina-
tion to join this fight in his advanced years. Perhaps he realized
that it was futile. When the constitution was at last revised, three
years after his death, the changes were so minimal that Virginia
continued to lag behind the North in its embrace of democratic
suffrage and representation.

Jefferson was even less willing to resume the assault on
slavery. The last gasp of his Revolutionary idealism had occurred
during his presidency when, in his annual message of December
1806, he recommended legislation to abolish the African slave
trade. The Constitution, as a result of what one historian has

called a "dirty compromise" over commerce and the slave trade, prohibited Congress from abolishing the slave trade prior to 1808. This was a concession to the delegates from South Carolina and Georgia, who had threatened not to ratify the Constitution if the slave trade was not protected for a period of time. Jefferson, to his credit, recommended action as soon as Congress obtained the constitutional authority in order to "withdraw the citizens of the United States from all further participation in those violations of human rights which have been so long continued on the unoffending inhabitants of Africa, and which the morality, the reputation, and the best interests of our country have long been eager to proscribe." Congress quickly passed a law prohibiting the further import of slaves from Africa as of January 1, 1808.

That, however, was the most Jefferson was willing to do. While his powers in this regard were admittedly few, he might have lent the prestige of his office and his personal popularity to the cause of limiting slavery. His failure to support the move to prevent slavery in the Louisiana Purchase has already been noted. He might also have advocated the abolition of slavery in the District of Columbia, which was under the control of Congress. Nor did he extend diplomatic recognition to Haiti, where blacks set up an independent republic in 1804. Such a move would have encouraged colonization (the removal of blacks to the West Indies or Africa), which Jefferson considered as essential to any emancipation movement. His embrace of colonization itself reveals how far he had moved from the attempted objectivity toward blacks in the *Notes on Virginia*. Jefferson by 1815 had clearly come to the conclusion that blacks were inferior by nature and that they could not survive in a competitive society. Colonization was a way of ridding the country of both blacks and slavery. Even so, some American statesmen, such as Madison and Henry Clay, viewed colonization as the only politically feasible alternative to slavery, and they helped to form the American Colonization Society in 1817. Jefferson took no active role in it.

His record on manumission was no better. The burden of his debts might have prevented him from freeing slaves toward the end of his life, but he was not so encumbered while president, or in fact at any time prior to the panic of 1819. Jefferson freed only three slaves during his lifetime, an embarrassingly small number. The judgment of Merrill D. Peterson, one of his most judicious biographers, is apt: "At bottom he did not care enough to sacrifice himself, or even put himself to great inconvenience, for the freedom of slaves, certainly not in the declining years of life."

VIRGINIA HAD NEVER BEEN FRIENDLY TO Jefferson's reforms, least of all his 1779 scheme for public education, yet, ironically, education, particularly the establishment of a state university, became the "holy cause" of his retirement years. It was not a quixotic notion; a university was the one reform that stood a chance in the legislature. The southern states had pioneered the idea of secular, tax-supported universities in the years after the Revolution. Georgia and North Carolina had working institutions by 1800, and the University of South Carolina opened three years later. Midway through his presidency Jefferson outlined a plan for a university in Virginia at the request of a friend who thought the General Assembly might be receptive. Jefferson's concept was of an "academical village," with houses containing classrooms, interspersed with lodgings for students, and all structures connected by covered walkways. Although a proposal to establish a university was introduced into the assembly in 1806, nothing came of it.

In his retirement years Jefferson tackled the project more indirectly. Several of his neighbors were endeavoring in 1814 to establish a private secondary school, the Albemarle Academy, in Charlottesville, and they invited Jefferson to serve on the board. Jefferson had a generally low regard for such institutions. Petty academies of this kind, he told Adams, "commit their pupils to the theatre of the world with just taste enough of learning to be alienated from industrious pursuits, and not enough to do service in the ranks of science." Jefferson nevertheless accepted the invitation because he could see in the academy the germ of something better. In the fall of 1814, while the rest of the country mourned the burning of Washington, Jefferson drafted a petition to the legislature to change the name of Albemarle Academy to Central College.

He had learned in the legislative battles of the 1770s that political spadework was necessary before any of his reformist ideas could be made to flower. He could count on the support of the governor, his long-time friend and political ally, Wilson Cary Nicholas. Jefferson's point-man in the assembly was Joseph C. Cabell, scion of a family that had dominated the politics of neighboring Amherst County for half a century, and a leading member of the Senate. In January 1816, the assembly passed a bill, drafted by Jefferson, creating Central College. A Board of Visitors of only six men governed the college, and the governor followed Jefferson's suggestion that Madison, Monroe, and Cabell, as well as Jefferson himself be named to the board.

As self-appointed architect, Jefferson drafted plans for his "academical village," with pavilions that would house professors and simultaneously serve as classrooms separated by a "range" of individualized living quarters for students. At its first regular meeting on May 5, 1817, the Board of Visitors approved Jefferson's plan and authorized the purchase of 200 acres of land near Charlottesville for the site. Jefferson visited the site that summer, adjusted his plan to the lay of the land, and decided the locations of six pavilions. Under Jefferson's plan the pavilions and ranges lay in two parallel lines, facing one another. When Jefferson sent a copy of his design to Latrobe, the Capitol architect suggested placing a large building in the center of one side of the open-ended quadrangle. He gave Jefferson a sketch of a building with a Romanesque dome. Jefferson quickly agreed, telling Latrobe that the north end of the quadrangle would be filled with "something of the grand kind" if the legislature approved the idea of a state university.

Each of the visitors had donated $1,000, and Jefferson raised additional funds from Virginia friends. As a result, the cornerstone of the first pavilion was laid on October 6, 1817, with President Monroe officiating. However, public funds were necessary if the project was to succeed, and the General Assembly had never been receptive to the idea of state-supported education. In 1810 Shenandoah Valley Federalist Charles Fenton Mercer had coaxed the Assembly into establishing a Literary Fund, which provided a modest amount of taxpayers' money for the education of the poor. But that seemed to be the extent of the legislature's commitment. Jefferson, nevertheless, had never abandoned his concept of a statewide system with appropriate doses of learning for the laborers, the gentry, and the cognoscente. In the fall of 1817 he sent Cabell the draft of a bill for a comprehensive scheme of elementary, secondary, and higher education. After extended debate, the legislature rejected the bill. However Cabell salvaged what he could by adding to the annual Literary Fund appropriation an amendment providing $15,000 for the establishment of a state university once the legislature had determined its location. This passed both houses in February 1818 and marked the inception of the University of Virginia.

It was a victory mostly in form, for the appropriation was embarrassingly inadequate, and the legislature had not yet approved the location. (Both William and Mary and Washington College in Lexington were lobbying for the legislature's blessing.) Demonstrating shrewd political acumen when a project dear to his heart was involved, Jefferson made the most of it. The governor, James Preston, a large-minded Republican from the southwestern corner of the state, named him to the commission to recommend a location and loaded it with well-disposed members, such as Madison. The commission met in August 1818, approved the Charlottesville site, and adopted Jefferson's scheme of instruction. Jefferson proposed a faculty of ten professors, each responsible for a field of learning, such as ancient and modern languages, mathematics, natural history (science), and the law. Jefferson's concept broke completely with the traditional classical curriculum, still in use in the New England colleges, by embracing new fields of learning, such as chemistry, economics, and modern languages. It was unique in another way. Alone among universities in America or Europe, Jefferson's school would have no chair of divinity or religious studies. The constitutional principle of separation of church and state barred such a chair in a public institution, Jefferson said.

The University of Virginia was the culmination of Jefferson's lifelong effort to bring Enlightenment values to Virginia. The curriculum as well as the architecture reflected his love for rationalism. This engraving by Benjamin Tanner done around the time of Jefferson's death depicts the university's central library building and ranges.

The legislature approved the commission's report and formally established the University of Virginia in January 1819. The following December Jefferson reported to the governor that the walls of seven pavilions and thirty-seven dormitories (each housed two students) had been erected and $80,000 was needed to complete them. The legislature, its treasury empty because of the depression that struck that year, declined to vote the money, but it did allow Jefferson to borrow $50,000 from the Literary Fund (and then, years later, excused repayment). Jefferson was determined from the beginning that the architectural style be classical. "We are sadly at a loss here for a [volume of] Palladio," he had written Madison in 1817. All three of his editions had gone to Washington, and no one in Charlottesville had one. The pavilions Jefferson worked out were not Palladian, in fact, but pure Greek, the capitals of each representing a different order,

Doric, Ionic, and Corinthian, so that students received daily instruction from their very surroundings.

The "grand" building destined for the north side of the quadrangle Jefferson designed in 1821. Called the Rotunda, it was a scale model of the Pantheon in Rome. Mathematically proportioned, the horizontal (stairs and cornice) and vertical (columns) lines of the building literally squared a circle formed by the dome. Its public function was to be the university library. The much traveled scholar George Ticknor (credited with introducing to the United States the flower of German culture in the age of Beethoven and Goethe) visited Charlottesville in 1824 and pronounced Jefferson's serried mass of red bricks and white columns "more beautiful than anything architectural in New England, and more appropriate to a university than is to be found, perhaps, in the world."

Jefferson personally recruited the faculty, and that proved to be the most frustrating job of all. He had hoped to lure the finest collection of scholars in the nation, but none of the leading intellects of New England schools was willing to move to the backwoods of Virginia. Jefferson ultimately obtained most of the professors from England, and none were prominent scholars. The only Virginian named to the new faculty, George Tucker, then a member of Congress, was given the chair of moral philosophy.

The university opened without fanfare on March 7, 1825, with about thirty students in attendance. A few weeks later Jefferson wrote proudly that he was "closing the last scenes of life by fashioning and fostering an establishment for the instruction of those who are to come after us. I hope its influence on their virtue, freedom, fame, and happiness will be salutary and permanent." He remained active in the affairs of the university to the end of his life, attending his last board meeting only three months before he died. The University of Virginia was truly his eternal monument.

HAVING WITNESSED THE UNTIMELY DEATHS of his wife and all but one of his children, Jefferson was no stranger to tragedy. Yet, in some sense, one of the greatest tragedies of his life was that he himself lived too long. The future of the country and the coming generation were not what he had expected. His letters in the last decade of his life are punctuated with laments over "the rising generation, of which I once had sanguine hopes." The nation underwent dramatic change in the decade after the War of 1812, inspired in large measure by the liberal capitalism that had been at the root of Jefferson's own philosophy. Textile mills and iron foundries sprouted up everywhere in the northern states. Artisan shops that had once employed two or three journeymen now housed a hundred or more, and the employer, once a craftsman himself, had become a capitalist who spent his time counting costs, overhead, and profits. By the time Jefferson died labor unions were being formed in some trades, and cities like New York and Philadelphia were experiencing the first strikes by organized labor. Newly formed banks, easy credit, and paper money fueled these changes. A Second Bank of the United States, chartered by Congress toward the end of Madison's presidency, was the most profligate lender of all, until it found itself in trouble in the panic of 1819. Jefferson had never comprehended the mystery of banking. The paper money issued by banks, he wrote in 1816, was designed only "to enrich swindlers at the expense of the honest and industrious part of the nation."

Still a man of the eighteenth century in many ways, Jefferson felt overwhelmed by the paper-money business culture that had swept the country. Once again he began to fear the commercialization of the country with its historical corollaries, the love of luxury and corruption. The old Country party rhetoric crept back into his writings. He saw England as pacing the decline because George III and his wicked ministers had "spent the fee simple of the kingdom, under pretence of governing it; their sinecures, pensions, priests, prelates, princes, and eternal wars, have mortgaged to its full value the last foot of their soil."

He failed to understand American economic development in part because he had to view it from afar. Virginia, once the nation's leader in wealth, population, and intellect, had become an economic and cultural backwater. The Missouri controversy (1819–1821), in which northern congressmen mounted a public attack on the institution of slavery, brought home to Virginians that they no longer played a leadership role; they were in a minority, a maligned one at that. They retreated into a stale and doctrinaire defense of states rights, and Jefferson wound himself in the same cocoon. He objected to the Missouri Compromise, which declared that no slaves would be allowed in the Louisiana Purchase north of latitude 36° 30', on grounds that it would leave the Union permanently divided. "This momentous question," he wrote, referring to the controversy, "like a fire bell in the night, awakened and filled me with terror. I considered it at once as the knell of the Union." The criticism from the North also made him more defensive about slavery. He still favored emancipation in principle, but only if the freed blacks could be returned to Africa. "But as it is," he wrote, "we have the wolf by the ear, and we can neither hold him, nor safely let him go. Justice is in one scale, and self-preservation in the other."

He blamed the troubles of his state, as well as his own financial difficulties, on banks, paper money, and the tendency toward "consolidation" (i.e., the growth of federal power at the expense of the states). Leading the drift toward "consolidation" was Jefferson's old nemesis, Chief Justice John Marshall. In a series of decisions following the War of 1812 Marshall gave judicial blessing to the expansion of federal powers, upholding, for instance, the constitutionality of the Bank of the United States. Under Marshall's leadership the Supreme Court became an important agency in the shaping of national policy. Marshall's influence reawakened Jefferson's old fears of a politicized judiciary free of popular control. Writing to Old Republican Spencer Roane (a son-in-law and protege of Patrick Henry), he lamented: "We find the judiciary on every occasion, still driving us into consolidation. . . . The constitution . . . is a mere thing of wax in the hands of the judiciary, which they may twist and shape into any form they please."

Ill health and indebtedness contributed to his deepening

gloom. He suffered a serious illness in 1818, and he was never completely free from physical suffering thereafter. Debt threatened to drown him altogether. The War of 1812 had damaged him financially, but he still had extensive holdings in lands and slaves. American farmers generally prospered in the postwar years because there was a good market in Europe where the land had been savaged by decades of war. Virginia did not share in the prosperity, however. The year 1816 was one of severe drought, and the Hessian fly struck its grain crop the following year. In 1817 Jefferson harvested only enough wheat to seed the next year's crop. He had to borrow money simply to meet living expenses, which remained high because of his hospitality and taste for expensive wines. He could not sell his slaves without risking future impoverishment, and his lands had become all but worthless. Virginia's best and brightest were moving to the rich cotton lands of Alabama and Mississippi. Land was for sale everywhere, and there were no takers.

Jefferson managed to cope with the hard times until the panic of 1819 sent him skidding down the slope to poverty. The Bank of the United States, which had fed the postwar boom with an easy lending policy, found itself in trouble in mid-1818, and it reflexively put on the brakes. Jefferson learned what this meant when the bank's Richmond branch suddenly curtailed his credit by twelve percent. This meant that on his $3,000 loan he had to repay $375 of it at once. This, he said, "is really like a clap of thunder to me, for god knows I have no means in the world of raising money on so sudden a call, my whole and sole dependence being only in the annual income of my farm." The actions of the federal bank forced contractions by the Bank of Virginia, which also forced him to pay back part of a loan. He did so only by borrowing from yet another bank.

In the midst of the panic his old friend Wilson Cary Nicholas went bankrupt, and this administered the *coup de grace* to Jefferson's own fortune. In 1818 Jefferson had endorsed two notes, each for $10,000, representing loans to Nicholas by the Bank of the United States. Endorsing notes was a practice that dated from colonial times when Virginia had no banks. Nicholas had previously endorsed notes for Jefferson, and as governor, he had helped mightily in the founding of the University. The endorsement, moreover, seemed safe enough, for Nicholas was thought to be worth $300,000. Much of his wealth, however, was in worthless Virginia lands, and when the panic "revolutionized" his fortune, he defaulted on the notes. Jefferson, as first endorser, was liable, and to cover his obligation he once again mortgaged his Bedford plantation, Poplar Forest. The interest on that drained $1,200 from his annual income.

Although farm prices turned upward in 1821, Jefferson sank farther and farther into debt. An account in 1823 listed debts in the amount of $40,000 in addition to the $20,000 obligation incurred on Nicholas's account, and by the time he died his indebtedness exceeded $100,000. In the final year of his life Thomas Mann Randolph went bankrupt, leaving Martha and her unmarried children completely in Jefferson's care.

His last illness, a urinary infection, struck in May 1825 and caused him to spend long months on a couch of pain. In March 1826, knowing he would soon die, he made his last will. There was little he could bequeath, for he died knowing that even Monticello would have to be sold to pay his debts. He freed five slaves by his will; all were artisans whom he apparently felt stood a good chance of economic survival as freedmen.

In June Jefferson was invited to participate in the celebrations that were planned in Washington, D.C., for the fiftieth anniversary of the Declaration of Independence. He had to decline, but the occasion did inspire some thoughts about the meaning of the American experiment. "All eyes are opened, or opening to the rights of man," he wrote. "The general spread of the light of science has already laid open to every view the palpable truth that the mass of mankind has not been born, with saddles on their backs, nor a favored few booted and spurred, ready to ride them legitimately, by the grace of god." It was his final affirmation of faith in democracy. Yet the words were not his own. The metaphor of freedom from saddles and spurs came from the gallows testament of Colonel Richard Rumbold, hanged for his part in the Rye House Plot of 1685 against Charles II and his brother James. Rumbold's dying words were quoted in several of the Whig histories that graced Jefferson's library shelves. In his political philosophy he had come full circle; he died in embrace of English whiggery.

A physician who was professor of medicine at the university attended him in his last days. "Until the 2nd and 3rd of July," the doctor recalled, "he spoke freely of his approaching death; made all his arrangements with his grandson, Mr. Randolph, in regard to his private affairs; and expressed his anxiety for the prosperity of the University." By the third he was unconscious much of the time, although he awoke on that evening to ask, "Is it the Fourth?" He was told it soon would be. He died, as he wished, on the following day, the fiftieth anniversary of the Declaration of Independence. John Adams, who died on the same day, breathed his last with the words "Thomas Jefferson still lives." In a sense, he was right.

Jefferson was buried alongside his wife on the sloping hillside of Monticello. He had designed his own grave marker, a simple obelisk, and requested that his epitaph be "the following inscription and not a word more":

Here was buried
Thomas Jefferson
Author of the Declaration of American Independence
of the Statute of Virginia for religious freedom
and Father of the University of Virginia.

He explained that "because by these, as testimonials that I have lived, I wish most to be remembered."

When the perceptive Frenchman, Alexis de Tocqueville, visited the United States five years after Jefferson's death, he discovered a society that had sought "to evade the bondage of system and habit, of family maxims, class-opinion, and, in some degree of national prejudices." Tocqueville described for his readers how in Europe aristocracy bound all members of a community to one another, while New World democracy had severed every link in that chain. In America, Tocqueville noted, the individual stands alone without hereditary allies or neighborhood support. Personal freedom and economic opportunity—that was the gist of Jefferson's ideas and convictions. He did not fully understand what he had wrought, nor was he entirely comfortable with the result. It was his legacy nonetheless.

Suggested Reading

THE READER WITH AMPLE LEISURE TIME will find very rewarding the six-volume biography by Dumas Malone, *Jefferson and His Time* (Boston, 1948–1981). The best single-volume biography is still Merrill D. Peterson, *Thomas Jefferson and the New Nation* (New York, 1970). A more recent study, focusing largely on Jefferson's public career, is Noble E. Cunningham, Jr., *In Pursuit of Reason: The Life of Thomas Jefferson* (Baton Rouge, 1987). Those wanting a general overview of America in the age of Jefferson may turn to Norman K. Risjord, *Jefferson's America, 1760–1815* (Madison, 1991).

H. Trevor Colbourn, *The Lamp of Experience: Whig History and the Intellectual Origins of the American Revolution* (Chapel Hill, 1965) has an excellent chapter on the influence of Whig historians on the young Jefferson. The chief proponents of the thesis that Jeffersonian ideology was based on English whiggery are Lance Banning, *The Jeffersonian Persuasion: Evolution of a Party Ideology* (Ithaca, 1978) and Drew McCoy, *The Elusive Republic: Political Economy in Jeffersonian America* (Chapel Hill, 1980). The thesis that Jefferson was the godfather of liberal capitalism is set forth in Joyce Appleby, *Capitalism and a New Social Order: The Republican Vision of the 1790s* (New York, 1984); John R. Nelson Jr., *Liberty and Property: Political Economy and Policy Making, 1789–1812* (Baltimore, 1987); and Stephen

Watts, *The Republic Reborn: War and the Making of Liberal America, 1790–1820* (Baltimore, 1987).

Isaac Kramnick adds a new dimension to the Appleby thesis in his recent book, *Republicanism and Bourgeois Radicalism: Political Ideology in Late Eighteenth Century England and America* (Ithaca, 1990). Kramnick argues that Jefferson's intellectual debt was not to English Country party writers, but rather to the middle-class "radicals," such as Joseph Priestley and James Burgh, who were writing contemporaneously with the American Revolution and heralded the movement for parliamentary reform and free enterprise in Britain.

Bruce A. Ragsdale, "Non-Importation and the Search for Economic Independence in Virginia, 1765–1775" (Ph.D. diss., University of Virginia, 1985), a book soon to be published by Madison House, has provided an important new analysis of the motives of Revolutionary Virginians. I found that his thesis of economic independence blended well with the Appleby thesis, and my interpretation of Jefferson's political economy is much indebted to him.

A detailed study of Virginia politics after the Revolution and the role of Jefferson and Madison in party formation is Norman K. Risjord, *Chesapeake Politics, 1780–1800* (New York, 1978). The most thorough and judicious study of the 1790s is Stanley Elkins and Eric McKitrick, *The Age of Federalism* (New York, 1993). Noble E. Cunningham, Jr., *The Process of Government under Jefferson* (Princeton, 1978) is indispensable to understanding Jefferson's presidency.

Of the many monographs on particular aspects of Jefferson's life, two of the best and most recent are Frank L. Dewey, *Thomas Jefferson, Lawyer* (Charlottesville, 1986) and Charles A. Miller, *Jefferson and Nature: An Interpretation* (Baltimore, 1988).

In *Jeffersonian Legacies* (Charlottesville, 1993) Peter S. Onuf has assembled an excellent collection of the most recent scholarly assessments of Jefferson, ranging from his religious views to his attitudes toward slavery. William W. Freehling, *The Road to Disunion: Secessionists at Bay, 1776–1854* (New York, 1990) places

Jefferson's views on slavery in the context of antebellum southern thought.

Those wishing to sample the writings of Jefferson himself may turn to Merrill D. Peterson's single-volume *Thomas Jefferson: Writings* (New York, 1984) or Peterson, *The Portable Thomas Jefferson* (New York, 1977), while researchers will find invaluable the multi-volume *The Papers of Thomas Jefferson* edited by Julian P. Boyd, Charles T. Cullen, and John Catanzariti (Princeton, 1951–   ).

Index